JOHN

REFORMED EXPOSITORY BIBLE STUDIES

A Companion Series to the Reformed Expository Commentaries

Series Editors

Daniel M. Doriani
Iain M. Duguid
Richard D. Phillips
Philip Graham Ryken

1 Samuel: A King after God's Own Heart
Esther & Ruth: The Lord Delivers and Redeems
Song of Songs: Friendship on Fire
Daniel: Faith Enduring through Adversity
Matthew: Making Disciples for the Nations (two volumes)
Luke: Knowing for Sure (two volumes)
John: The Word Incarnate (two volumes)
Galatians: The Gospel of Free Grace
Ephesians: The Glory of Christ in the Life of the Church
Philippians: To Live Is Christ
Hebrews: Standing Firm in Christ
James: Portrait of a Living Faith

JOHN

THE WORD INCARNATE
Volume 1 (Chapters 1–10)

A 13-LESSON STUDY

REFORMED EXPOSITORY
BIBLE STUDY

JON NIELSON
and **RICHARD D. PHILLIPS**

P U B L I S H I N G
P.O. BOX 817 • PHILLIPSBURG • NEW JERSEY 08865-0817

© 2022 by P&R Publishing

All rights reserved. No part of this book may be reproduced, stored in a retrieval system, or transmitted in any form or by any means—electronic, mechanical, photocopy, recording, or otherwise—except for brief quotations for the purpose of review or comment, without the prior permission of the publisher, P&R Publishing Company, P.O. Box 817, Phillipsburg, New Jersey 08865–0817.

Scripture quotations are from the ESV® Bible (*The Holy Bible, English Standard Version*®), copyright © 2001 by Crossway, a publishing ministry of Good News Publishers. Used by permission. All rights reserved.

All boxed quotations are taken from Richard D. Phillips's *John*, vol. 1, in the Reformed Expository Commentary series. Page numbers in quotations refer to that source.

ISBN: 978-1-62995-927-6 (pbk)
ISBN: 978-1-62995-928-3 (ePub)

Printed in the United States of America

CONTENTS

Series Introduction   7

Introducing John   9

Lesson 1: The Eternal Word (John 1:1–18)   15

Lesson 2: Following the Lamb of God (John 1:19–51)   23

Lesson 3: Rejoicing and Rebuke (John 2:1–25)   31

Lesson 4: Born Again through Faith in the Son of God (John 3:1–36)   39

Lesson 5: Living Water (John 4:1–54)   47

Lesson 6: The Authoritative Son (John 5:1–47)   55

Lesson 7: The Bread of Life (John 6:1–36)   63

Lesson 8: Teaching That Divides (John 6:37–71)   71

Lesson 9: Not Yet Time (John 7:1–36)   79

Lesson 10: The Light of the World (John 7:37–8:20)   87

Lesson 11: Greater Than Abraham (John 8:21–59)   95

Lesson 12: Blindness to Sight (John 9:1–41)   103

Lesson 13: The Good Shepherd (John 10:1–42)   111

SERIES INTRODUCTION

Studying the Bible will change your life. This is the consistent witness of Scripture and the experience of people all over the world, in every period of church history.

King David said, "The law of the Lord is perfect, reviving the soul; the testimony of the Lord is sure, making wise the simple; the precepts of the Lord are right, rejoicing the heart; the commandment of the Lord is pure, enlightening the eyes" (Ps. 19:7–8). So anyone who wants to be wiser and happier, and who wants to feel more alive, with a clearer perception of spiritual reality, should study the Scriptures.

Whether we study the Bible alone or with other Christians, it will change us from the inside out. The Reformed Expository Bible Studies provide tools for biblical transformation. Written as a companion to the Reformed Expository Commentary, this series of short books for personal or group study is designed to help people study the Bible for themselves, understand its message, and then apply its truths to daily life.

Each Bible study is introduced by a pastor-scholar who has written a full-length expository commentary on the same book of the Bible. The individual chapters start with the summary of a Bible passage, explaining **The Big Picture** of this portion of God's Word. Then the questions in **Getting Started** introduce one or two of the passage's main themes in ways that connect to life experience. These questions may be especially helpful for group leaders in generating lively conversation.

Understanding the Bible's message starts with seeing what is actually there, which is where **Observing the Text** comes in. Then the Bible study provides a longer and more in-depth set of questions entitled **Understanding the Text**. These questions carefully guide students through the entire passage, verse by verse or section by section.

It is important not to read a Bible passage in isolation, but to see it in the wider context of Scripture. So each Bible study includes two **Bible Connections** questions that invite readers to investigate passages from other places in Scripture—passages that add important background, offer valuable contrasts or comparisons, and especially connect the main passage to the person and work of Jesus Christ.

The next section is one of the most distinctive features of the Reformed Expository Bible Studies. The authors believe that the Bible teaches important doctrines of the Christian faith, and that reading biblical literature is enhanced when we know something about its underlying theology. The questions in **Theology Connections** identify some of these doctrines by bringing the Bible passage into conversation with creeds and confessions from the Reformed tradition, as well as with learned theologians of the church.

Our aim in all of this is to help ordinary Christians apply biblical truth to daily life. **Applying the Text** uses open-ended questions to get people thinking about sins that need to be confessed, attitudes that need to change, and areas of new obedience that need to come alive by the power and influence of the Holy Spirit. Finally, each study ends with a **Prayer Prompt** that invites Bible students to respond to what they are learning with petitions for God's help and words of praise and gratitude.

You will notice boxed quotations throughout the Bible study. These quotations come from one of the volumes in the Reformed Expository Commentary. Although the Bible study can stand alone and includes everything you need for a life-changing encounter with a book of the Bible, it is also intended to serve as a companion to a full commentary on the same biblical book. Reading the full commentary is especially useful for teachers who want to help their students answer the questions in the Bible study at a deeper level, as well as for students who wish to further enrich their own biblical understanding.

The people who worked together to produce this series of Bible studies have prayed that they will engage you more intimately with Scripture, producing the kind of spiritual transformation that only the Bible can bring.

Philip Graham Ryken
Coeditor of the Reformed Expository Commentary series

INTRODUCING JOHN

The gospel of John is one of the world's true treasures. It contains many of the sayings that are most memorable and blessed to God's people. The book is so simple that children memorize their first verses from its pages and so profound that dying adults ask to hear it as they pass from this life. It is said that John is a pool safe enough for a child to wade in and deep enough for an elephant to drown in. Martin Luther wrote, "This is the unique, tender, genuine, chief Gospel. . . . Should a tyrant succeed in destroying the Holy Scriptures and only a single copy of the Epistle to the Romans and the Gospel according to John escape him, Christianity would be saved."[1]

Although this gospel does not specify its **author**, we can be sure of his identity from both internal and external evidence. The book claims to be written by an eyewitness and disciple of Jesus (21:24). We know from the other gospels that the disciples closest to Jesus were Peter, James, and John. Of these, only John is never named in this gospel—which is hard to explain apart from the author's modesty concerning himself. In his place we are told of a "beloved disciple" who is evidently both the author and the apostle John. The early church affirms this view. Irenaeus, a second-century bishop who knew people who had personally known John, attests that John, "the disciple of the Lord," wrote this gospel in Ephesus, and his view is backed up by every ancient document that addresses the subject.[2]

We do not know the exact **date** when John wrote his book. It is traditionally thought to be the last of the four gospels to be composed. Some

---

1. Quoted in James Montgomery Boice, *The Gospel of John*, vol. 1, *The Coming of the Light: John 1–4* (Grand Rapids: Baker Books, 1999), 13.
2. Irenaeus, *Against Heresies*, 3.1.1, trans. W. H. Rambaut, in *The Apostolic Fathers with Justin Martyr and Irenaeus*, The Ante-Nicene Fathers 1, ed. A. Cleveland Coxe (repr., Peabody, MA: Hendrickson, 1999), 414.

scholars place its writing before the destruction of the temple in AD 70. But the consensus holds that John wrote it no earlier than AD 80 and perhaps as late as the AD 90s.

Although we must surmise the gospel's author, its **main purpose** is clearly stated: "These are written so that you may believe that Jesus is the Christ, the Son of God, and that by believing you may have life in his name" (20:31). John is sometimes called the "gospel of belief," because it was written to inspire faith in Jesus and his gospel. Specifically, it tells us that we are to believe that "Jesus is the Christ, the Son of God" and also that, through faith in him, we receive "life in his name." Given this statement of purpose, we may approach the gospel of John as especially communicating these two precious themes.

The first **theme**—the gospel of John's overwhelming presentation of Jesus as the Son of God—makes it widely recommended to those who are looking for an introduction to the Christian faith. Its opening lines refer to Jesus as "the Word" who in the beginning was "with God" and "was God" (1:1). Then, toward the end of the book, the disciple Thomas believes and falls before Jesus, after his resurrection from the dead, crying, "My Lord and my God!" (20:28). In between these two poles, the book presents numerous claims of Jesus's deity. John's prologue in chapter 1 describes Jesus's incarnation in terms of Isaiah 7:14's promise regarding *Immanuel* ("God with us"): "The Word became flesh and dwelt among us, and we have seen his glory, glory as of the only Son from the Father, full of grace and truth" (1:14). Joined with John's teaching about Jesus's deity is his equal insistence on the doctrine of the Trinity, since Jesus is "the only God, who is at the Father's side" and "has made him known" (1:18).

After John's prologue comes what scholars refer to as the "Book of Signs" (1–11), which consists largely of Jesus's miracles. These further display his deity. Jesus turns water into wine in John 2; performs miraculous healings in John 4, 5, and 9; feeds more than five thousand people with a few loaves and fish, then walks on water, in John 6; and raises Lazarus from the grave in John 11. His claim to deity brings him into conflict with the religious authorities, which leads him to make even clearer statements regarding his divine nature. For instance, when Jesus tells the Jewish leaders, "Before Abraham was, I am" (8:58), he deliberately takes God's most sacred self-revelation and applies it to himself (see Ex. 3:14).

John's gospel is known for its seven famous "I am" sayings. Jesus associates his ministry with God's gift of manna to Israel in the desert: "I am the bread of life" (6:35). He sets himself forth as the true source of divine blessing: "I am the light of the world" (9:5). He is "the door" (10:9), "the good shepherd" (10:11), "the resurrection and the life" (11:25), "the way, and the truth, and the life" (14:6), and "the true vine" (15:1). These claims are clear and bold, and by them we learn how Jesus brings God's saving grace to a world that is lost in sin.

Connected to the theme of Jesus's divinity is the idea that he is "the Christ." The Greek word *Christos* is a translation of the Hebrew *Meshuach*: the long-awaited Messiah of God's people. This word means "anointed one" and refers to the three anointed offices that Jesus came to fulfill: prophet, priest, and king.

- Jesus is the true prophetic revelation of God's being and character. By his gracious nature, righteous deeds, and saving words, Jesus reveals God to all the world: "Whoever has seen me has seen the Father" (14:9).
- Jesus also comes as the true King of God's people, in the line of his earthly father, David. When the Roman governor Pontius Pilate claims authority over Jesus, Jesus replies to him, "My kingdom is not of this world" (18:36)—referring to the kingdom of heaven.
- Jesus comes as the Priest who cleanses believers from their sins by offering himself as their true atoning sacrifice. The second main portion of John's gospel, known as the "Book of the Passion" (12–21), records the events surrounding Jesus's crucifixion and his glorious resurrection from the grave.

Jesus the Christ fulfills the work of the prophets by revealing God through his own life. He restores kingly rule over God's redeemed people, and he ministers as the true Priest by shedding his own blood, just as John the Baptist predicted (see 1:29).

If the first part of John's purpose is to persuade us that Jesus is "the Christ, the Son of God," the second part, and second theme, is to show that we receive eternal life through personal faith in Jesus. The most well-known verse in John—and perhaps the whole Bible—eloquently states this gospel truth: "For God so loved the world, that he gave his only Son, that whoever believes in him should not perish but have eternal life" (3:16). The appeals that the book contains about taking up personal faith in Jesus start with Jesus's call to his disciples in John 1. After Jesus's first miracle, we read that "his disciples believed in him" (2:11). Jesus says that "the Son of Man [must] be lifted up [on the cross], that whoever believes in him may have eternal life" (3:14–15). God the Father invests Jesus with the authority to save, and so Jesus declares, "Whoever hears my word and believes him who sent me has eternal life. He does not come into judgment" (5:24). Again and again, John connects personal faith in Jesus to forgiveness of sins and eternal life.

In addition to the themes of Jesus's deity and our salvation through faith, John includes additional content that is absent from Matthew, Mark, and Luke. In particular, the early chapters of his gospel provide more scenes from Jesus's ministry of evangelism, as the Savior calls disciples to trust and follow him. John provides new information about Jesus's calling of the disciples and follows it with his nighttime encounter with the Pharisee Nicodemus, during which Jesus tells him, "You must be born again" (3:7). Particularly uplifting is Jesus's saving encounter with an unnamed woman by a well, whom Jesus offers the "living water" of spiritual life (4:10; see also v. 14). When the woman believes, she immediately tells the people of her village about Jesus, and they too believe. Like this woman, readers are motivated and instructed to spread the gospel by Jesus's command at the book's conclusion: "As the Father has sent me, even so I am sending you" (20:21).

Further new material consists of Jesus's Farewell Discourse in John 13–16, followed by his High Priestly Prayer in John 17. In these chapters, John provides great detail about Jesus's last meal with his disciples on the night of his arrest. After humbly washing their feet, Jesus discusses at length the provision of the Holy Spirit after Jesus has departed from the world. In John 17, one of the most remarkable and informative chapters of the entire Bible, Jesus prays to the Father for his church as he stands on the brink of surrendering himself to the cross. As we listen to the Son of God praying for us, we stand like Moses on holy ground, filled with astonished adoration as Jesus's love for our souls is revealed.

As do Matthew, Mark, and Luke, John narrates the details of Jesus's atoning death and glorious resurrection, but this book again provides a wealth of material that is not found elsewhere. The world, in all its malice, conducts a false trial to legitimize Jesus's murder. Pilate, who represents the authority of man's kingdom, cynically consigns Jesus to death despite his clear innocence. Jesus is presented to the Jewish crowd in a "crown of thorns and [a] purple robe" (19:5)—in mockery of his divine claims—and Pilate affixes a sign to his cross that reads, "Jesus of Nazareth, the King of the Jews" (v. 19). As Jesus dies on the cross for our sin, he cries aloud glorious words of victory—"It is finished" (v. 30)—before giving up his life. After he rises from the grave on the third day, he meets with Mary Magdalene and "doubting" Thomas, among others, to present them with his resurrection body. The book concludes with Jesus's tender pastoral ministry to Simon Peter, as he graciously gives him the commission "Feed my sheep" (21:17).

Countless readers have discovered the truth about Jesus and his gospel in the pages of John. It is, in fact, Jesus himself whom we meet in this book, through the ministry of God's Holy Spirit and the words of inspired Scripture. Jesus himself promises you that if you believe in him and read this gospel in faith, "you will know the truth, and the truth will set you free" (8:32).

Richard D. Phillips
Coeditor of the Reformed Expository Commentary series
Coeditor of the Reformed Expository Bible Study series
Author of *John* (REC)

LESSON 1

THE ETERNAL WORD

John 1:1–18

THE BIG PICTURE

Matthew, Mark, and Luke—which are often referred to as the *Synoptic* Gospels—share many accounts, organizational structures, and themes. The gospel of John stands apart from them by providing many unique insights into the incarnation, life, teaching ministry, signs, death, and resurrection of Jesus Christ, the Son of God. In this lesson, we will study John's thoroughly theological introduction to his gospel.

In these opening eighteen verses, John echoes the opening verses of the Bible as he presents Jesus as the eternal "Word" of God, who is eternally existent, coequal with God the Father, and active in the creation of the universe (1:1–3). This Word came as the "light" in order to shine in a world that is dark with sin and rebelling against its Creator (1:4–5). John then introduces the prophetic ministry of John the Baptist, who, as the final prophetic witness to the Son of God and light of the world, preceded Jesus and heralded his coming (1:6–8). After this, we are told that many will sinfully reject Jesus, when he comes, but that some will believe and be saved by him—and will thus take on the privilege of being "children of God" (1:9–13).

John concludes his introduction by explaining the theological significance of Jesus's incarnation. The eternal Word took on flesh and dwelt in the midst of God's people (1:14–18). Through Jesus, the eternal God of the universe has made himself known to sinners, who can find grace when they believe in him.

16 The Eternal Word

Read John 1:1–18.

GETTING STARTED

1. Have you studied the gospel of John in detail before? If so, what about the book encouraged you the most? What aspects of it were challenging or confusing?

2. What tends to confuse people about the identity and person of Jesus Christ—especially as they concern his incarnation and his existence during eternity past?

OBSERVING THE TEXT

3. How would you describe the tone, style, and approach of the opening verses of John's gospel? What seem to be the most important points he is communicating?

> **A Theological Introduction, pg. 7**
> John differs from the other Gospels in many ways, among them the manner by which he begins his account of Jesus. Like the other Gospel writers, he wants us to understand that Jesus is God made flesh—the very God who became truly man. . . . John's prologue gives a theological explanation for Jesus' coming into the world, beginning with his eternal origin before the creation of all things.

4. What aspects of Jesus Christ's coming to earth does John emphasize in these first eighteen verses? What do we learn from them about Jesus's identity? What do we learn about human beings?

5. Who else appears, and is named, in these opening verses, and what role does he have in relation to Jesus Christ?

UNDERSTANDING THE TEXT

6. The opening verses of this passage shape the way we understand Jesus Christ as a member of the Trinity (1:1–3). In what sense is he distinct from God the Father? And yet how do these verses make it clear that he is also fully and completely God?

> **What Is Saving Faith? pg. 45**
> If faith in Christ is the great distinction, we should want to know what faith is. John 1:12 gives a definition: "All who did receive him, who believed in his name." Faith, then, involves believing and receiving Jesus Christ as he has revealed himself—in his person and saving work.

7. What is the significance of the imagery of "light" and "darkness" that we see in 1:4–5—and how does this imagery echo the opening verses of Genesis?

8. What do we learn about John the Baptist in 1:6–8? What additional details are we given about him in 1:15? Why do you think the apostle John establishes what John the Baptist's role is as his gospel begins?

9. How do many people in the world respond to the Word (1:9–11)? What about their response is surprising, sad, or ironic? How do you think John intends us to view this response?

10. John gives us eternally and gloriously good news in 1:12–13. What is the right way to respond to the light that has come into our world? What blessings come to those who respond this way?

11. What was an important consequence of the fact that Jesus came in the "flesh" to dwell in the midst of God's people (1:14)? What contrast does John again draw between the ministry of Jesus and the role of Moses (1:15–17)? What does the Word ultimately and fully communicate to human beings (1:18)?

BIBLE CONNECTIONS

12. Read Genesis 1:1–3. What close echoes of these opening verses of the Bible do you see in the opening verses of John's gospel? What is John communicating about Jesus by including them?

13. While we are beginning our study of the gospel of John, take a moment to read John 20:31—which is often identified as John's "purpose statement" for why he composed this gospel. What does John want his readers to know and believe about Jesus? Why does he want them to know and believe this?

THEOLOGY CONNECTIONS

14. As we saw on page 9 of the introduction, Martin Luther called John "the unique, tender, genuine, chief Gospel" and wrote, "Should a tyrant succeed in destroying the Holy Scriptures and only a single copy of the Epistle to the Romans and the Gospel according to John escape him, Christianity would be saved." Why do you think Luther would have held such a high view of this particular gospel? What is unique about the opening eighteen verses of John in comparison with the opening lines of the other three gospels?

15. Answer 21 of the Westminster Shorter Catechism explains that Jesus Christ, "being the eternal Son of God, became man, and so was and continues to be, God and man in two distinct natures, and one person, forever." What about Jesus Christ changed at the moment of his incarnation? What remained, and still remains, unchanged about the second person of the Trinity?

> **Give Yourself Wholly, pg. 41**
> Do we receive Christ wholeheartedly, gratefully, and publicly? Or are we too enamored of the world to let it know that we have been saved out of it? Thank God that salvation is by grace alone and that there is forgiveness for our sin. But let us be grateful and receive Jesus as his people should, giving ourselves wholly to him.

APPLYING THE TEXT

16. How does John's introduction to his gospel serve to elevate your view of Jesus and your understanding of his glory and his eternal identity? In what ways should your worship and admiration of Jesus Christ be deepened by this passage?

17. Why should you be grieved by the fact that so many of Jesus's "own" rejected him? What should this grief spur you to do?

18. What effect does the reality of the incarnation have on your appreciation of the condescension, mercy, and grace God has shown to sinners?

PRAYER PROMPT

As you come to the end of this first lesson, take a few moments to praise God for the amazing revelation of himself that he shared by sending his Son, Jesus Christ, in the flesh. Thank him for sending Jesus to dwell in our midst as one who is fully God and fully man. Praise him for the gift of salvation that he offers, by grace and through faith, to all who will believe in him.

LESSON 2

FOLLOWING THE LAMB OF GOD

John 1:19–51

THE BIG PICTURE

John follows up the theological introduction to his gospel with a description of the witness of John the Baptist that's more substantive than the mention we saw in our last lesson. As he baptizes and prepares the people, John the Baptist bears clear, humble, and faithful witness to Jesus (1:19–28). When representatives from the Jewish leaders come to question him, John acts in his role as Christ's final prophetic forerunner and points away from himself and to the coming Messiah.

Next, we are introduced to Jesus himself. When he comes out to meet John the Baptist in the wilderness (1:29–34), the prophet immediately identifies him as the Lamb of God—the one to whom his entire ministry and baptism have been pointing (vv. 29–31). John the Baptist then describes the way the Holy Spirit authenticated Jesus's life and ministry and identifies him as the "Son of God" who will baptize with the Holy Spirit (vv. 32–34).

In the remainder of this lesson's passage, Jesus begins to call disciples to follow after him (1:35–51). Andrew and Peter are called first, and Andrew immediately identifies Jesus as the "Messiah"—or "Christ" (vv. 35–42). After next calling Philip, Jesus calls Nathanael, who is initially skeptical due to Jesus's inauspicious hometown, Nazareth (vv. 43–46). Nathanael is amazed, however, by Jesus's knowledge of him—and is quickly convinced that he is the "Son of God" and the "King of Israel" (vv. 47–51).

By the time the first chapter of John's gospel concludes, we have seen the clear, collective witness of both John the Baptist and Jesus's first disciples: that Jesus is the Son of God, the Messiah, and the long-awaited King of God's people!

Read John 1:19–51.

GETTING STARTED

1. Why are we endeared to people who willingly give credit to others and seek to make others look good? What type of quality does this require—and why do some people fail to do this?

2. Have you ever been in a mentoring relationship or been trained by someone to perform a task or to serve in a certain role? What challenges did this involve? What kind of attitude did you need to adopt in order to learn and be trained effectively?

Two Aspects of Christian Discipleship, pg. 97
When we come to Jesus and begin truly to follow him, we enter into a second aspect of Christian discipleship. First, we come seeking forgiveness of sin and salvation with God. But then we begin a lifelong course of study under Jesus' teaching.

OBSERVING THE TEXT

3. John the Baptist consistently points away from himself, and to Christ, as he is peppered with questions from the Jewish leaders. What does John's motivation, throughout this passage, seem to be?

4. What surprises you about the initial responses that Jesus receives from the men who become his first disciples? What questions do they have? What seems to excite them about Jesus's identity and the opportunity for following him?

5. How does this passage continue to prove this gospel's point that Jesus is the Son of God and the promised Messiah?

> **We Are Not Witnesses to Ourselves, pg. 78**
> It is important for us to follow John's example in refusing to focus our witness on ourselves. John was a witness to the Savior, not a savior himself. This is essential for us to remember and emulate. Our lives and ministry are to attract people's attention, but the danger is that we would allow them to focus their admiration on us. . . . These must not take the place of our witness to Christ.

UNDERSTANDING THE TEXT

6. What can we conclude about the motivation of the Jews who come to interrogate John the Baptist (1:19–27)? What information do they want from him? What might be making them suspicious of him and of the powerful ministry he is performing in the wilderness?

7. The Pharisees' questions, in 1:19–23, suggest that they have a sense of John the Baptist's importance and significance. Who do they think he might be, and how does he respond when they voice this? What comparison does he make, in 1:25–28, between himself and the One who will come after him?

8. John's witness regarding Jesus becomes more doctrinally precise in 1:29. What do his words in this verse reveal about Jesus? What images from the Old Testament—images with which the Jewish people would be quite familiar—do John's words evoke?

9. According to John the Baptist, how were Jesus's identity and purpose confirmed (1:30–34)? What is important about this confirmation? What does it reiterate about the One who will come after John the Baptist?

10. What do the ways in which Andrew and Simon (Peter) immediately react to Jesus imply about what they have expected, and longed for, regarding the Messiah (1:35–41)? What do you think the fact that Jesus names Simon implies about the role he plays in Peter's life (1:42)?

11. What do Philip's words tell us about him (1:43–45)? What does Nathanael's reaction to Philip's announcement suggest about the general reputation of the town of Nazareth (1:46)? What does Jesus do in 1:47–51 to reveal to Philip and Nathanael that his identity is the Son of God—and what hint does he give them about what is to come once they follow him?

> **The Mark of a Thriving Christian, pg. 89**
> A healthy, spiritually thriving Christian is one who . . . never tires of glorifying Jesus as "the Lamb of God, who takes away the sin of the world," and who also exults, "He took away my sin as well."

BIBLE CONNECTIONS

12. Read Exodus 12:1–13, which describes the institution of the Feast of Passover. When the Jewish people in the wilderness heard John refer to Jesus as the "Lamb of God," they would have had passages like this in mind. What does this allusion that John the Baptist makes tell us about Jesus?

13. While John records the calling of only the first four disciples, in this passage, we know that Jesus ultimately gathers twelve followers to himself, who will serve as his closest friends and trainees. Why is this number significant? What do you think Jesus is communicating to God's people by gathering twelve men to be his disciples?

THEOLOGY CONNECTIONS

14. John the Baptist's weighty statement that Jesus Christ is the "Lamb of God, who takes away the sin" of God's people points to the most central aspect of Christ's work: his substitutionary death on the cross. Why is it important that we not see this act as being peripheral to his other work and ministry?

15. According to answer 42 of the Westminster Larger Catechism, Christ is called the "Mediator" because "he was anointed with the Holy Ghost above measure, and so set apart, and fully furnished with all authority and ability, to execute the offices of prophet, priest, and king of his church." What does our passage for this lesson show us about the ways in which Jesus was set apart through his anointing?

APPLYING THE TEXT

16. How could you better follow John the Baptist's example in the area of your own gospel witness? What seems to motivate him—and what motivates you?

17. What aspects of the first disciples' immediate reaction to Jesus challenge and convict you? How can you follow their example as a disciple of Jesus today?

18. What is beautiful and compelling about the way Jesus interacts with these first disciples? How can this passage serve to deepen your love and admiration for the King and Savior you follow today?

PRAYER PROMPT

As you close your study of this passage, ask God to embolden your witness for Jesus Christ. Pray that he would give you both the courage and the humility to point others away from yourself—and toward the glorious and gracious Savior. Then ask him to give you a humble heart and a willingness to follow after Jesus as his loyal disciple, to take him at his word, and to commit to worshiping him alone.

LESSON 3

REJOICING AND REBUKE

John 2:1–25

THE BIG PICTURE

John 2 opens with a wedding celebration at Cana in Galilee—the setting for Jesus's first miraculous sign (2:1–12). As Jesus participates in the wedding festivities along with his mother and his disciples, the wedding host runs out of wine (v. 3). After his mother speaks to him about it, Jesus steps forward to perform his first sign: changing the water in six stone jars into fine wine—finer wine than anything that was being served earlier! John explicitly calls this the first of Jesus's "signs," through which we will see him manifest his glory, and the disciples respond to it by believing in him (v. 11).

The tone of the narrative changes as John next depicts Jesus's fiery encounter with the Jews and money changers in the temple's courts in Jerusalem (2:13–22). As Jesus violently confronts those who have turned this place of worship into a place of trade, in verses 13–17, his "zeal" for God's house brings to his disciples' minds the prophetic words of Psalm 69. When the Jews demand a sign that will prove the authority he has for these actions, Jesus points to a great sign that lies ahead: that his body (the "temple") will be raised back to life after three days (vv. 18–22).

The chapter concludes with commentary from John on Jesus's unwillingness to "entrust" himself to people, even as many begin to believe that he is the Son of God because of the powerful signs he is performing (2:23–25). The Messiah has now begun his public ministry: he is performing signs that point to his identity, confronting the sin and corruption of the worship taking place in Jerusalem, and inviting the faithful belief of his true disciples—who not only are drawn to the signs but truly follow the Savior.

Read John 2:1–25.

GETTING STARTED

1. Describe a positive transformation—whether physical, emotional, or spiritual—that you have experienced in your own life or witnessed in the life of someone you know. What emotions accompanied this transformation?

2. Why are religious hypocrisy and corruption particularly damaging to the witness of the church? Describe a time when you saw someone within the church confront these things well.

> **Belief and Disbelief, pg. 140**
> [John] tells us that while there were different responses to Jesus, Jesus had one response to all people: "Jesus on his part did not entrust himself to them, because he knew all people and needed no one to bear witness about man, for he himself knew what was in man" (John 2:24–25). The Greek text contains a deliberate parallel: they believed in Jesus' name when they saw his signs, but he did not believe in them; that is, Jesus did not believe in their supposed "belief."

OBSERVING THE TEXT

3. John begins to use the language of "signs" throughout this passage. What does he use this word to mean? What seems to be the purpose of the signs he describes?

4. What reaction do the disciples have to Jesus throughout this chapter? As it comes to a close, what responses do we see other people having to him—and how does Jesus address these responses?

5. What are we learning about Jesus's chief concerns and purposes throughout this passage? How does he respond to those who look to him for help? What makes him angry?

UNDERSTANDING THE TEXT

6. What do you think is significant about the fact that Jesus's *first* sign is transforming water into wine (2:1–11)? What deeper spiritual realities might this miracle be hinting at—and why should it fill us with hope?

7. John gives us some additional explanation of Jesus's first sign in order to help us to interpret it (2:11). What does he say that Jesus is doing through this miraculous sign? In what way do his disciples react to this sign?

8. What have the money changers and merchants in 2:13–17 done to corrupt the place of worship in Jerusalem—and how does Jesus react to them? What does he say to explain the specific cause of his righteous indignation (v. 16)?

9. What sign does Jesus mention to the Jews who interrogate him in 2:18–22? What misunderstanding do they evidence—and what does the gospel writer explain that Jesus actually means by what he says?

10. What seems to be different about the belief of Jesus's disciples (2:22) compared to the belief of the many people who are in Jerusalem during the Passover Feast (2:23)? Why do the masses "believe" in Jesus? What does Jesus's reaction tell us about the nature of such belief (2:24–25)?

11. What do this first sign and prophecy explain to us about Jesus's purpose for coming? In what ways is John already inviting us to look forward to the cross of Jesus Christ—and to the empty tomb?

BIBLE CONNECTIONS

12. Read Matthew 9:14–17, and note the wine metaphor that Jesus utilizes to describe his ministry. What additional insight do these verses offer into the way that wine symbolizes the newness and transformational nature of Jesus's coming into the world?

13. Read Mark 11:17 and Isaiah 56:1–8, and pay particular attention to verse 7. What vision for the nations do we see in the Isaiah passage? How have the money changers and merchants in our passage for this lesson interfered with this goal?

> **Transformation, pg. 127**
> John identifies this event as a sign, so it speaks of a greater spiritual reality. Surely the point is that Christian salvation involves a transformation of our lives. Just as he turned water into wine, Jesus tells us, "Unless one is born again he cannot see the kingdom of God" (John 3:3).

THEOLOGY CONNECTIONS

14. Many commentators have pointed out that Jesus chose to perform his first miraculous sign at a wedding. What do you think this choice implies?

15. It seems that some people can display a kind of "belief" that Jesus does not see as valid (2:24–25). The Westminster Confession of Faith explains that "the principal acts of saving faith are, accepting, receiving, and resting upon Christ alone for justification, sanctification, and eternal life, by virtue of the covenant of grace" (14.2). With that in mind, what would you say fickle and shallow belief is marked by?

APPLYING THE TEXT

16. What picture does Jesus's first sign portray of the gospel's impact on a believer? What does it suggest about how Christ views you and responds to your need?

17. In what way should we be challenged and confronted by the righteous anger and indignation Jesus shows toward those who have made the place of worship in this passage into a place of trade and greed? Over what do you think Jesus would confront our worship today? What things tend to distract us from purely and faithfully worshiping our God?

18. How can you be sure that you are truly following Jesus with saving faith, rather than simply participating in a church culture or in Christian fellowship? What are some signs of genuine belief, conversion, and devotion to Jesus Christ?

His Body, Our Temple, pg. 137
We see what Jesus meant, then, when he referred to his own body as the temple. It is his death on the cross that serves as the place where sin is forgiven and where man is received into God's grace. Have you come to the cross? Have you confessed your sin and looked to Jesus as the Lamb of God, slain for you?

PRAYER PROMPT

This passage introduced us to Jesus's initial sign—changing water into wine—as well as his prophecy that his body would be destroyed and then rebuilt in three days. Today, ask God to grant you the faith to believe the truths to which these acts point! Pray for belief in Jesus—the one who brings miraculous transformation to sinful hearts and lives. Ask God to help you to place your faith solely in Jesus's sacrificial death on the cross and his glorious resurrection from the dead!

LESSON 4

BORN AGAIN THROUGH FAITH IN THE SON OF GOD

John 3:1–36

THE BIG PICTURE

John 2 concluded by putting on display the fickle and shallow "belief" that many in the crowds displayed in response to Jesus's signs. Verse 24 told us that Jesus did not "entrust" himself to these people, but he encouraged his disciples to put their faith in him and acknowledge that he is the Son of God. Now, in John 3, we see Jesus taking time to help one religious leader to move from a partial understanding of his identity to full, saving belief in him.

Nicodemus, a Pharisee, comes to speak to Jesus under cover of night, probably for fear of his fellow religious leaders (3:1–15), and immediately struggles to grasp Jesus's teaching about how he must be "born again" by the Spirit in order to come into the kingdom of God. Jesus then uses images from the books of Ezekiel and Numbers to illustrate a person's need for new birth—for conversion—which is dependent not on one's ethnic heritage but on the saving work God has done by the Spirit's power through the work of the Son (vv. 9–15). Although different Bible translations handle the next passage in different ways, many commentators hold that Jesus's conversation with Nicodemus concludes here and that 3:16–21 is an additional theological explanation from the apostle John, which says that God manifested himself in the sending of Jesus the Son, in whom sinners must believe in order to receive eternal life. To reject Jesus—the "light"—is to remain in sin, rebellion, and "darkness."

Jesus and his disciples then set out for the countryside (3:22), and the remainder of the chapter focuses on John the Baptist. His disciples, who have noted Jesus's rising popularity—and how the crowds have been turning to him and away from John the Baptist—approach him with their concern about this (3:23–26). John the Baptist's response is humble and Christ-honoring; he again exalts Jesus and embraces his own role as a witness to one who is far greater than he (3:27–30). The chapter concludes with more explanation from the gospel writer: Jesus came from heaven and was sent by God the Father, and everyone needs to believe in the Son of God in order to receive eternal life (3:31–36).

Read John 3:1–36.

GETTING STARTED

1. In what context (or contexts) have you heard the words "born again"? What connotations—whether positive or negative—can this phrase carry?

2. What aspects of devotion to Jesus and to God's Word tend to be embarrassing culturally for people today? What particular Christian beliefs are considered old-fashioned, irrelevant, or problematic?

We Decrease for Christ, pgs. 202–3

[John the Baptist] saw that his ministry must give way to that of Christ. In the same way, Christians who are useful and make a difference in this world are resolved to make little of themselves so that Christ will be exalted, believed, and followed.

OBSERVING THE TEXT

3. When confronted by a Jewish religious leader who ought to understand the miraculous means of God's salvation, what attitude does Jesus display? What encouragement can this middle-of-the-night conversation give to those who struggle with a lack of understanding or with doubt?

4. Why do you think John the apostle chooses to provide additional commentary on the conversations he records? What truths does he further explain and apply to his readers by doing so?

5. What might have been a temptation for John the Baptist at this stage in his ministry? How does he show, once again, that he is not building his own platform and ego?

UNDERSTANDING THE TEXT

6. What do you notice about the way Nicodemus approaches Jesus (3:1–9)? What is his attitude as he does so? What sets him apart from the other Jewish religious leaders? And how does Jesus respond to him?

7. Why is it so difficult for Nicodemus to grasp what Jesus is teaching him about his need of being "born again" (3:1–8)? What is Jesus implying about what this Pharisee lacks—despite his great training, learning, and familiarity with the law of God?

8. Jesus continues his explanation to Nicodemus in John 3:10–15. What reference does he make in order to depict himself as the key object of faith? Why do you think Jesus implies that Nicodemus should already understand these truths about salvation—and what might this tell us about the way we, too, should read the Old Testament?

9. John 3:16 is one of the most frequently quoted verses of the entire Bible. What do we learn from that verse about the significance of Jesus's coming and about what our response to him should be? And if this stretch of verses is John's commentary, rather than Jesus's dialogue, why do you think it appears here—directly after Jesus's nighttime conversation with Nicodemus?

> **New Birth Is Possible, pg. 162**
> Nicodemus might not have been born again and therefore might not have been able to understand. But his questions were sincere, and starting in verse 14, Jesus gave him a glorious answer. How can one be born again? Jesus' first answer was that the new birth is possible because of the *sacrifice of the Son of Man*.

10. What wrong and sinful responses to Jesus are described in 3:17–21, and what imagery is used to portray those responses? In what way do these verses continue to emphasize the themes of John's gospel?

11. What does John the Baptist do in John 3:22–30 to demonstrate tremendous humility? What truths about Jesus's coming and identity does the gospel writer repeat in 3:31–36? What do those verses tell us is the only right response to Jesus Christ, the Son of God?

BIBLE CONNECTIONS

12. Read Ezekiel 36:22–28 and 37:1–10, and consider the references Jesus makes to the Spirit and the wind in John 3:5–8. What is he teaching this Jewish religious leader about true conversion and salvation? According to Jesus, how is a person saved—and why is belonging to the Jewish people not enough?

13. Read Numbers 21:4–9. How did God use the bronze serpent as a means of saving his people? Why do you think Jesus is using this historical picture to invoke what he will do—and the means through which he will do it?

THEOLOGY CONNECTIONS

14. A. W. Pink writes, in reference to Nicodemus, "The fact that a preacher has graduated with honors from some theological center is no proof that he is a man taught of the Holy Spirit. No dependence can be placed on human learning."[1] Why is Bible training and learning helpful—and even essential—for God's people? And yet why must we be careful not to depend on such training for salvation?

15. Answer 89 of the Westminster Shorter Catechism explains that "the Spirit of God makes the reading, but especially the preaching of the Word, an effectual means of convincing and converting sinners, and of building them up in holiness and comfort, through faith, unto salvation." List the ways in which Jesus aims to convince, convert, and build up Nicodemus in this passage.

---

1. Arthur W. Pink, *Exposition of the Gospel of John* (Grand Rapids: Zondervan, 1975), 124, quoted in Richard D. Phillips, *John*, vol. 1, *Chapters 1–10* (Phillipsburg, NJ: P&R Publishing, 2014), 161.

APPLYING THE TEXT

16. If Nicodemus, a highly trained teacher of the Jewish law, needed to be "born again" by the Spirit of God in order to enter the kingdom, then that is certainly the case for all of us—no matter our background, religious training, or church affiliation! Consider your own life. What evidences do you see of the Spirit's work in your conversion?

17. What dangers and warnings do we see in this passage for those who reject the Son of God and choose to remain in darkness? What should our reaction to these warnings be? Why should we come away from them feeling stirred up to more courageously and compassionately proclaim the gospel?

> **Eyes Open, pgs. 180–81**
> At the beginning of this chapter, Jesus described faith as "seeing." . . . Faith is having our eyes open so that we see Jesus for who he is. This reminds us that until we are born again we cannot and do not believe, because our sinful nature is opposed to faith. Therefore, to realize that you believe in Christ—that you accept what the Bible teaches, trust it as your own saving truth, and personally commit yourself to Jesus—is to have wonderful good news. It means that you have been born again.

18. John the Baptist's statement in John 3:30 serves as a kind of "motto" for the Christian life. What would living out this motto look like in the areas of our obedience, service, and gospel witness? What gets in the way of your desire to see Jesus "increase"—and your willingness to allow yourself to decrease?

PRAYER PROMPT

This passage again shows us that Jesus's identity is the Messiah and the promised Son of God, and it calls us to embrace him with saving belief—to be "born again" by the power of the Holy Spirit. If you trust and love Jesus today, God has done a miraculous saving work in your heart—praise him for that! Then, ask God to make you more humbly willing to point *away* from yourself to the life-giving hope found in Jesus Christ, the Son of God.

LESSON 5

LIVING WATER

John 4:1–54

THE BIG PICTURE

As Jesus had his midnight conversation with Nicodemus in John 3, we saw this Jewish religious leader being confronted with a surprising reality: that he needed to be "born again," by the Spirit and through faith in the Son, in order to enter the kingdom of God. Despite his great learning and training, Nicodemus was lost without supernatural and saving faith in Jesus—the Son of God! Now, in John 4, we are introduced to a very different type of character: a Samaritan woman, whom Jesus engages in conversation at a well during the heat of the day.

For Jesus to even talk to a woman—and to a *Samaritan* woman, at that—is a cultural taboo for a Jewish religious teacher of the day, such as him. Yet Jesus earnestly engages this woman and directs her to the saving belief she needs to have in him—the Messiah (4:1–26). This conversation begins with Jesus helping the Samaritan woman to realize her need for "living water" that will satisfy her eternally (vv. 7–15). He then moves on to expose her sexual sin and the many relationships she has had with men—which leads her to abruptly switch the subject to ceremonial worship (vv. 16–24). When the conversation turns to the promised Messiah, Jesus finally declares to the woman, "I who speak to you am he" (v. 26).

Jesus tells his disciples that he is accomplishing the work of the Father and reaping a harvest; and in fact, his investment in the woman leads many to come to faith in him while he is staying in this Samaritan town (4:27–45).

Jesus then travels to Cana in Galilee, where he performs another sign: the healing of the sick son of an "official" from a distance (4:46–54). John notes that this is the second sign Jesus has performed in Galilee, as he continues to bear witness to his identity as the Son of God.

Read John 4:1–54.

GETTING STARTED

1. Do you ever think that certain "kinds" of people are beyond salvation—and even beyond hope? Why? What makes such thinking contrary to the gospel? What view does it take of the saving power of God?

2. What cultural boundaries hold you back from sharing the gospel more regularly with unbelievers today? What are you trying to avoid when you choose *not* to speak up about the faith and hope you have in Jesus?

> **The Gospel Is for Everyone, pgs. 216–17**
> It is particularly interesting to compare and contrast Nicodemus, featured in John 3, with the woman at the well in John 4. Nicodemus was a man at the top of life, admired by almost everyone, but one who needed to be born again. Lest we think that only the proud need salvation, however, we are next introduced to someone at the other end of life. . . . John placed these two figures side by side to show that the gospel is for everyone.

John 4:1-54   **49**

OBSERVING THE TEXT

3. Contrast the woman at the well in Samaria with Nicodemus, the Pharisee from John 3—in what ways are they different? How does Jesus demonstrate care and concern for this woman? In what ways does he confront her, as well?

4. How does Jesus's interaction with this woman change her—and what impact does this change have on the people of the surrounding town and area?

5. What amazing sign does Jesus perform in 4:46-54? How does the official demonstrate his faith—and what detail about this healing serves to prove its miraculous nature and further bolsters this official's faith in Jesus?

> **The True Place of Worship, pg. 261**
> A new answer is given to the Samaritan woman's question about where to worship. "On this hill or in Jerusalem?" she asked. Jesus answered, "I AM." As Moses was called to the burning bush, Jesus now calls us to himself as the true place of worship. Wherever we are, we may come directly to God through faith in Christ.

UNDERSTANDING THE TEXT

6. After Jesus enters Samaria and sits down beside a well (4:1–6), what do we learn in 4:7–9 that helps us to understand why the conversation that follows is unexpected and surprising? What does Jesus's interaction with this woman tell us about the gift of salvation that he offers—and about those whom he intends to receive it?

7. Jesus uses the metaphor of "water" in 4:10–15. What does the woman think he is talking about? What is he actually referring to?

8. When Jesus demonstrates his divine knowledge of this woman's life (and her sin), she redirects the conversation to the topic of worship (4:16–20). What does Jesus explain to her about God's coming salvation and its relationship to the Jewish people (4:21–24)? How does he say that true followers of God must worship him? What explicit statement does Jesus then make about his identity (4:25–26)?

9. In John 4:27–39, Jesus's disciples return to him at the well and the woman testifies about Jesus to the people in her town. What do verses 29–30 and 39 say is the result of her witness and testimony? How do verses 41–42 illustrate Jesus's metaphor about the "harvest" in verses 31–38?

10. Jesus returns to Galilee in 4:43–45, and in 4:46–47 he is confronted by an official whose son is ill. How does Jesus's initial remark cast doubt on the sincerity of this man's belief (4:48)? What relation does this have to a theme that we saw in John 2?

11. How does the official respond when Jesus questions his faith—and then to the promise Jesus gives him afterward (4:49–52)? How does Jesus demonstrate his authority and power, and what is the result of the sign he performs (vv. 53–54)? What makes this result similar to what we saw happening in Samaria earlier in this chapter?

BIBLE CONNECTIONS

12. Read Genesis 12:1–3, which records the initial promise God made to Abram, the father of the Jews. What support does this passage lend to Jesus's insistence in John 4:22 that salvation is "from the Jews"? But what does it say to show that salvation is not *limited* to the Jews, as well?

13. Read the invitation found in Revelation 22:17. What is encouraging about this verse? What does it mean, in practical terms, for sinners to "come" and "take the water of life"—and through whom can they do this?

THEOLOGY CONNECTIONS

14. Although Jesus clarifies to the Samaritan woman that salvation comes from the Jews (since the Messiah will come from the Jewish kingly line), he also downplays the importance that Jerusalem or any other "holy" mountain will have in the future (4:21). Why do Jesus's death and resurrection eliminate the need for God's people to gather in order to worship him in a specific geographical location? What allows sinners to now gather anywhere in the world and rightly worship the true and living God?

15. Answer 56 of the Heidelberg Catechism tells us that Christians can declare that "God, for the sake of Christ's satisfaction, will no more remember [their] sins, neither [their] sinful nature, against which [they] have to struggle all [their] life long." What attitude does the Samaritan woman in John 4 demonstrate when she realizes that Jesus knows all that she has ever done—and that he will no longer "remember" any of it? What makes this a beautiful illustration of how the gospel frees us?

APPLYING THE TEXT

16. What do we learn about Jesus's compassion and grace through the encounters he has in this passage with the Samaritan woman and the Galilean official? How do the insights this gives us into his gracious and gentle heart encourage us to come to him for help and forgiveness?

A Public Admission, pg. 272

It seems that [the Samaritan woman] was an immoral woman who was shunned by her neighbors, so the subject of her sinful past would surely have been a sore subject with her. But now, instead of being ashamed of her past, she blurts out that Jesus knows all about it. This is one of the most important signs that a person has come to faith in Christ: instead of covering his or her sin and resenting the subject, the true Christian publicly admits to sin . . . in order to show that Jesus is the Savior of sinners.

17. We've seen that the Samaritan woman's belief in Jesus became almost contagious throughout her town and area. Have you ever witnessed this type of infectious testimony for Jesus Christ? What does the Samaritan woman's behavior inspire, challenge, or instruct you to do in the area of your own witness?

18. How can the official's insistence, as he talks to Jesus (4:47, 49), inspire us regarding the way we should approach God in prayer? What warning should we take, from Jesus's initial words to him, about fickle belief that is tied only to signs and wonders (4:48)?

PRAYER PROMPT

In both Samaria and Galilee, Jesus's ministry and signs result in the saving *belief*, from people around him, in the Son of God and Savior of sinners. Praise God that his mercy comes both to sinful Samaritan women and high-ranking officials! As you close your study of this chapter of the gospel of John, pray for God to remind you that his gracious salvation is for everyone who will repent, turn, and place their faith in Jesus Christ, his Son. Pray that you will be able to boldly witness to others about this Savior of sinners who has shown mercy to you.

LESSON 6

THE AUTHORITATIVE SON

John 5:1–47

THE BIG PICTURE

As we have already seen in this study, John's chosen label for Jesus's miraculous works is "signs." These signs demonstrate Jesus's *identity* and *authority* and invite all who witness them to believe in him and receive eternal life. In the passage for this lesson, Jesus reinforces the fact that he is the Son of God who works on behalf of God the Father. As Jesus's opponents continue to object to his authority, Jesus explicitly tells them that his Father has sent him and bears ongoing witness to his identity and role.

We begin in Jerusalem, where Jesus miraculously heals a paralyzed man near a pool in Bethesda—only to be criticized by the Jewish leaders for performing this healing on the Sabbath (5:1–17). In response, Jesus links his own ongoing saving work to the ongoing work of his Father (v. 17). By calling God his Father, Jesus makes himself "equal" with God, and John interjects to explain that this is what drives the Jews' desire to put him to death (5:18).

The remainder of the chapter records an extended section of Jesus's teaching. First, he describes the authority he possesses as one who has been sent by God the Father (5:19–29). Next, he details the "witness" given to his identity by John the Baptist (5:30–35), by the miraculous signs and wonders that he himself is performing (5:36), and by God the Father through his Word that has been revealed throughout the generations (5:37–47). Jesus's claims are unmistakable: he is the unique and authoritative Son of God, and the Father has borne witness to his identity in multiple ways and committed to him the authority to speak, save, and judge. We must believe the words of Jesus and follow him in faith!

Read John 5:1–47.

GETTING STARTED

1. What objections have you encountered to the doctrine of Jesus Christ's divinity? What are other popular ways that people think about Jesus instead of recognizing his divinity?

2. In what settings do we typically see witnesses today? What makes the role of a witness important?

OBSERVING THE TEXT

3. What does Jesus do in this passage to continue to reveal his identity and purpose?

4. What opposition does Jesus face in this passage? What objections do his opponents raise against him—and what does he do that seems to make them feel most angry and threatened?

5. What massive claims does Jesus make in this chapter of Scripture? What argument do they offer to those who say that Jesus never presented himself as anything more than a human moral teacher?

UNDERSTANDING THE TEXT

6. How does Jesus's healing of the paralyzed man by the pool again show us his heart of compassion, kindness, and grace (5:1–9)? What can we learn from this incident about the salvation Jesus brings—and what does this healing reveal about what happens to sinners who turn to Jesus in faith?

The Son of God, pg. 315
Jesus'... claims to be God's Son were not blasphemous because God the Father desires to be worshiped through the worship of his only Son. Jesus states that the Father has appointed him as Judge, "that all may honor the Son, just as they honor the Father. Whoever does not honor the Son does not honor the Father who sent him" (John 5:23). This is why it is essential that we believe on God's Son, Jesus Christ.

7. What makes the Jews so angry in this passage (5:10–17)? What does their anger reveal about their hearts? How does Jesus respond to their anger, and what instructions does he give the man he has healed?

8. What explanation does John give in 5:18 for the Jews' desire to kill Jesus, and what does this reveal about their understanding of Jesus's claims? What has the Father done for the Son, according to John 5:19–24?

9. Jesus claims in 5:25–29 to hold power and authority over the hearts and souls of all human beings. How do these verses make it clear that Jesus is fully God? What role will Jesus have in judgment, according to these verses?

10. What different people and methods does Jesus say God the Father has used to bear witness to Jesus's identity and purpose (5:30–47)? Why do you think Jesus finds it important to describe these different types of witnesses, given the response the Jews have had to his public ministry and teaching thus far?

11. What does Jesus teach us in 5:39–47 about the right way for us to understand the Old Testament in relation to himself? What would it look like for our study of the Old Testament Scriptures to be guided by these verses?

BIBLE CONNECTIONS

12. Read the account of Jesus's baptism contained in Matthew 3:13–17. What example do you see in this story of the witness that the Son says the Father bears about him in John 5:37–38?

13. Jesus tells the Jewish leaders that Moses "wrote of" him. Read Deuteronomy 18:15, 18. What details about the Son does Moses give in this prophetic witness to him?

> **The Threat to Works-Religion, pg. 301**
> What really mattered [to the Jews] was not this stupendous act of divine grace, but that by carrying his mat on Saturday the man was violating the rules. I can think of few instances that better illustrate how works-religion opposes the grace of God. So driven were these leaders by the whip of legalism that this wonderful sign of God's grace was seen only as a threat.

THEOLOGY CONNECTIONS

14. Richard Phillips explains that the situation of the people who were at the pool in Bethesda reflects the spiritual condition we are in apart from Christ: "Just as they were physically disabled, we are spiritually disabled."[1] What do you think it means for humans to be "spiritually disabled"? What effect does this metaphor have on the way you understand our need for a Rescuer?

15. What does Jesus say in this passage to make it clear that God the Son is distinct from God the Father—and why is it important for us to affirm that these persons of the Godhead are distinct from each other and have different roles? What does Jesus say in this passage to make it clear that God the Father and God the Son are *equal* to each other and are both fully God—and why is it important for us to affirm the complete divinity of both the Father and the Son?

---

1. Richard D. Phillips, *John*, vol. 1, *Chapters 1–10* (Phillipsburg, NJ: P&R Publishing, 2014), 293.

APPLYING THE TEXT

16. What encourages you about Jesus's healing of the paralyzed man by the pool? How does the way he responds to the paralyzed man contrast with the way he interacts with the Jewish leaders in John 5:37–47? What can this teach you about the kind of attitude that is right to bring to Jesus?

17. Jesus's claims in this passage call us to hold on to the doctrine of his uniqueness and exclusivity. What does this doctrine mean? What makes it so central to Christian faith?

18. This passage presents Jesus as being fully divine, the giver of life, and the coming judge—how should you respond to this picture of your King? How is this passage serving to inform your worship of Christ and your awe before him?

> **The Ultimate Issue, pg. 337**
> Jesus presents himself to us today, just as the Jewish leaders received in person his claims to deity. It was true for them then, as it is true for us now, that questions or concerns about John the Baptist, about miracles, or about divine revelation matter little compared to him. What ultimately matters is simply this: What do we make of Jesus Christ? This is the ultimate issue in life and in death; everything else pales before it.

PRAYER PROMPT

As you close your study of this passage, thank God for the clear witness he has given you regarding the identity, person, and work of Jesus Christ, his Son. God's Word is not difficult to understand; its claims concerning Jesus are clear! Ask God for the humility to be able to look to Jesus in faith, belief, and repentance, trusting that he will one day be lifted high as the King and judge of all people.

LESSON 7

THE BREAD OF LIFE

John 6:1–36

THE BIG PICTURE

As we saw in the introduction, unique to John's gospel are the "I am" statements that Jesus makes throughout this narrative. Jesus uses these statements to identify himself with God and to show the ways that he is fulfilling the Old Testament prophecies and promises about the Messiah. John's gospel often pairs one of these "I am" statements with a miraculous sign that illustrates it and lends credence to Jesus's weighty claims. Such is the case in the passage that we will study in this lesson.

Every gospel writer records Jesus's miracle of feeding a group of five thousand men (not to mention women and children). As the others do, John describes the great crowd that gathers to hear Jesus's teaching, the lack of food that's available to feed such a crowd, Jesus's miraculous multiplication of five loaves of bread and two fish in order to feed the entire group, and the twelve baskets of leftover food that are then gathered afterward (6:1–15). Uniquely, though, John also tells of the crowd's desire to make Jesus king by force, which leads him to withdraw from them (v. 15).

After Jesus performs another miracle by walking on the water to join his disciples (6:16–21), the crowds finally catch up with him the next day (vv. 22–25). In the substantive teaching he delivers once they do (6:22–36), Jesus points them to the eternal and fulfilling "bread from heaven" that will provide them with lasting sustenance. Then, using the words God had used to reveal himself to Moses ("I AM"—Ex. 3:14), he makes a grand claim in response to the people's continued questions: "I am the bread of life" (v. 35). Ultimately, Jesus intended for his miraculous feeding of the crowd to point to himself (rather than to focus on physical food) and to display the need for sinners to come to him, believe in him, and feed on him by faith so that they will never be spiritually hungry again.

Read John 6:1–36.

GETTING STARTED

1. What do people in your culture today seem to *hunger* for—whether physically, emotionally, or spiritually? What do people turn to in their attempts to satisfy their hunger for these things?

2. Few people seem to reject Jesus entirely. What aspects of Jesus have you seen people embrace even if they deny the *divine* aspect of his identity? What areas of his teaching fit most conveniently and easily with the beliefs and norms of your broader culture?

OBSERVING THE TEXT

3. How does John make it clear that the crowd's motivation for continually seeking Jesus is shallow and misguided (6:1–2, 26)? Where in this gospel have we already seen this type of motivation turning up?

4. In 6:22–36, what connection does Jesus draw between the miraculous sign he has performed and his ongoing claims and teaching about his identity? What does the crowd seem to assume he means by what he is saying?

5. What aspects of Jesus's purpose and identity is he clarifying through the miraculous signs and teaching that we see in this passage? What has Jesus come to accomplish? What does he offer sinful human beings?

UNDERSTANDING THE TEXT

6. Describe the miraculous sign that Jesus performs in the opening section of this chapter (6:1–13). What elements of this miracle does John choose to describe? What does he leave up to our imaginations as we read?

The Answer to Our Every Need, pg. 353
Christ the true Redeemer conquers our foes—Satan, death, and the bondage of sin. Christ the true Passover Lamb covers us with his blood so that God's holy wrath passes us by. Christ the new Moses leads us through the wilderness of this life so that we meet with God, hear his Word, and become his holy people.... This is why we hunger and need to be fed. The miracle of his feeding of the five thousand shows how able Jesus is to meet our every need.

7. What do the people do after they see Jesus perform this sign (6:14)? What does Jesus then do in response to this—and what does this tell you about how well the people understand his kingship (6:15)?

8. In 6:16–21, how does Jesus further reveal his identity to his disciples? How do they initially react to what he does, and why? What does this sign prove about his power and authority?

9. Jesus sees through the motives of the people who have followed him and caught up with him (6:22–28). What does he say about their motives? What does he say should be their motivation instead?

10. As Jesus calls the crowds to believe, what connection does he draw between his coming and the manna that God gave to the Israelites, through Moses, in the wilderness (6:29–34)? What surprise twist does Jesus introduce in verse 33?

11. What massive claim does Jesus make in 6:35? What does he promise to those who come to him by faith? How have the crowds responded to him thus far (6:36)?

BIBLE CONNECTIONS

12. Read Psalm 23, and note the images David uses to portray God's loving care. What connection do you see Jesus drawing, in this lesson's passage, between himself and the divine Shepherd of Psalm 23? What does this tell us about his relationship with his people?

13. In Exodus 16:8–18, we read about how God initially provided manna—bread from heaven—for his grumbling and hungry people. Read through those verses now. What can we learn from this passage by reading it in light of Jesus's description of himself as "bread" from heaven that will give "life" to the world (John 6:33)?

> **Put It All in the Hands of Jesus, pg. 365**
> What motive will cause you to minister to those around you at work, in your families, in your neighborhoods, and around the world? It can only be the love of God in Jesus Christ. Should you not be burdened with compassion for the worldly and spiritual needs of those around you? . . . Take what you have, what you can do, and put it all in Jesus' hands.

THEOLOGY CONNECTIONS

14. Answer 168 of the Westminster Larger Catechism explains that, in the Lord's Supper, Christ's "death is showed forth; and they that worthily communicate feed upon his body and blood, to their spiritual nourishment and growth in grace." How do the sign and the teaching that Jesus gives us in this passage prefigure the Lord's Supper, during which we "feed" on him by faith? (We will continue to examine how Jesus's teaching in John 6 connects with the Lord's Supper in the next lesson, as well.)

15. Many Christians throughout the history of the church have struggled with how faith relates to works. How does the statement Jesus makes in John 6:29 help us to understand the right place to begin a life of obedience and service to God? Why is it important for us to begin here?

> **Missing the Point, pg. 376**
> If we think Jesus was pleased by this pursuit, we are surprised to find that he was not. The reason is that the people had failed to grasp the point of Jesus' miracle. It is true that Jesus fed them out of compassion for their physical needs. But the miracle was not intended merely to show Jesus as a provider of consumer goods and services. The point was to reveal him as the Son of God to whom they should look for their souls' salvation.

APPLYING THE TEXT

16. What has this passage told you about how you must seek to satisfy your deepest hunger, longings, and need? What have you learned about how you should relate to Jesus?

17. In the opening narrative of this passage, a boy contributes five loaves and two fish for Jesus's use. In what ways do you see this illustrating the service that we ourselves offer to God? What makes this an encouraging picture for weak people like us?

18. What approaches to Jesus that we see in this passage result in his withdrawal—and even his rebuke? What does the passage teach us is the right way to respond to him?

PRAYER PROMPT

As you close your study of John 6:1–36 today, begin your prayer by praising God for the compassionate care he has shown you through Jesus Christ, his Son. Thank him for graciously providing for you—not only materially but, as you put your faith in Jesus, eternally and spiritually as well. Pray for God to give you the grace to "feed" on Jesus by faith—to nourish your soul first and foremost through your faithful belief in him. Then ask him to help you as you participate in his gospel ministry—even while facing your own weakness and limitation.

LESSON 8

TEACHING THAT DIVIDES

John 6:37–71

THE BIG PICTURE

As Jesus continues to expand on the grand messianic statement from our previous lesson, this lesson's passage makes it very clear that people will react in very different ways to his authoritative claims: some will believe in him and find eternal life... and others will reject him, turn away in disbelief, and forfeit his salvation. Jesus, the Son of God, brings the good news of the hope that can be obtained only through him—but his is teaching that *divides*. Not everyone is able to accept the massive claims of this Messiah or submit to his demands for full faith and complete allegiance.

Jesus reasserts the close relationship he has with God the Father, who has sent him from heaven to give "life" to all who believe in him (6:37–40). This leads to more grumbling from Jesus's Jewish opponents, who seek to use his upbringing to discredit his claims; Jesus responds to them by again describing himself as the "living bread" from heaven, which all who desire eternal life must consume (6:41–51). Again the Jews take his statements very literally and wonder how this can be possible (6:52). Jesus doubles down as he calls all who would believe in him to feed on his flesh and drink his blood in order to have eternal life (6:53–59). The Jews cannot grasp that Jesus means that true believers will feed on him through their repentance and saving faith—which his sacrificial death on the cross makes it possible for them to do.

Finally, we switch gears as Jesus spends the remainder of the chapter talking with his disciples about the aspects of his teaching that they, too, find difficult (6:60–65). In fact, John notes that many disciples from Jesus's broader group turn back from following him at this point (6:66). The twelve disciples remain with him, though, and Simon Peter voices their belief that Jesus is speaking the words of "eternal life" to them (6:67–69). Jesus affirms that he has chosen them to be his disciples—but the passage ends with the revelation that one of his disciples, Judas, not only will turn away, as others have, but will ultimately betray him (6:70–71).

Read John 6:37–71.

GETTING STARTED

1. What aspects of the Bible, or of the Christian faith, tend to be most confusing to the unbelievers whom you know? Which of its truths or teachings tend to be most out of step with the popular culture of today?

2. Have you ever been confused about the meaning of the Lord's Supper? What has confused you? What different teachings or emphases have you encountered in different churches regarding this meal?

> **The Offering on the Cross, pg. 425**
> [Jesus'] flesh is the bread "that I will give for the life of the world" (John 6:51). This is why Jesus' words about his "flesh" and "blood" are associated with the Lord's Supper, since they both point to the same thing: Jesus' atoning death on the cross.

OBSERVING THE TEXT

3. Jesus develops his metaphor of "eating" his body and "drinking" his blood throughout this passage. What similar and related phrases does he repeat in order to draw out these themes?

4. What starkly different responses to Jesus's claims, invitations, and teachings do you see in this passage? Who gives these different responses?

5. What aspects of Jesus's teaching in this passage become too much for some of the Jews—and even for some of Jesus's closest disciples? Why do you think some of them turn back from following him after this speech?

> **Greater Than Moses, pg. 433**
> If we ask what it was about Jesus' teaching that so offended his hearers, the answers are many. First, Jesus did not satisfy their worldly desires; while they wanted baked goods, he kept talking about bread for the soul. Second was the insinuation that Jesus was a figure greater than the Jews' revered Moses. Compared to the manna that came through Moses, Jesus is "the true bread from heaven" (John 6:32).

UNDERSTANDING THE TEXT

6. What else does Jesus say in 6:37–40 about the close relationship he has with God the Father? What does he tell us in these verses about the sovereign role God plays in human salvation?

7. What seems to cause the Jews to start grumbling against Jesus in 6:41–42? What does Jesus imply about their spiritual condition (6:43–44)? What new angle does Jesus take as he continues his speech from 6:45–51?

8. Which point from Jesus is the next to make the Jews confused (6:52)? What does he then say to make his teaching more explicit—and what does he call people to do (6:53–59)?

9. What is the right way to understand Jesus's teaching from 6:53–59 in light of his sacrifice on the cross? What is the spiritual meaning of the "eating" of his flesh and "drinking" of his blood that Jesus says is required for eternal life?

10. Even Jesus's own disciples become disillusioned and divided by his teaching (6:60–66). What criticism of it do they offer? What does Jesus already know about the different responses people will have to his claims, signs, and teaching (vv. 63–65)? What separates those who believe Jesus from those who reject him (v. 65)?

11. Why does Simon Peter say that he (and the other disciples) will keep following Jesus (6:67–69)? What is revealed to readers about Judas—and what harsh label does Jesus give to him (6:70–71)?

BIBLE CONNECTIONS

12. Read Isaiah 8:14–15. According to these verses, what impact does the Word of God, and God himself, have on many people? How does our passage from John show us this prophecy being fulfilled?

Salvation Depends on God Alone, pg. 417
Conversion to Christ is a supernatural work that relies on God's power alone. "No one can come to me," Jesus said, "unless the Father . . . draws him" (John 6:44). And it is because salvation depends utterly on the inward working of God's sovereign grace that we know that the glory for our salvation goes to God alone.

13. In 1 Corinthians 11:23–26, Paul explains what he has "received" and passed on to the church with regard to the Lord's Supper. What more do these verses explain regarding Jesus's teaching, from our passage for this lesson, about his body and blood? With what attitude is this spiritual meal to be taken—and why?

THEOLOGY CONNECTIONS

14. Richard Phillips explains that the doctrine of *unconditional election* "teaches that apart from anything commendable in themselves, a people has been chosen by God to come to Christ and be saved. This 'election,' or 'choosing,' took place in eternity past."[1] What does Jesus say to confirm this in John 6:37–39? How do the ways that Jesus's hearers respond to his difficult teaching in this lesson's passage show us this doctrine being played out?

---

1. Richard D. Phillips, *John*, vol. 1, *Chapters 1–10* (Phillipsburg, NJ: P&R Publishing, 2014), 395.

15. The Westminster Confession of Faith says this about the Lord's Supper: "Worthy receivers, outwardly partaking of the visible elements in this sacrament, do then also inwardly by faith, really and indeed, yet not carnally and corporally, but spiritually, receive and feed upon Christ crucified, and all benefits of his death: the body and blood of Christ being then, not corporally or carnally, in, with, or under the bread and wine; yet, as really, but spiritually, present to the faith of believers in that ordinance" (29.7). How does this explanation help us to make sense of Jesus's words about eating his flesh and drinking his blood? Why is it important for us to understand that he means this in a spiritual—rather than physical—sense?

APPLYING THE TEXT

16. What is understandable about the Jews' objections to Jesus's teaching about eating his flesh and drinking his blood? Why do you think this made even some of his disciples turn away from following him? What does this tell us to expect when we proclaim God's Word and share its more difficult and countercultural teachings?

17. What promises does Jesus make, throughout this passage, to those who "eat" and "drink" of him and believe that he is the one sent from God the Father? What encouragement can you take from these promises as you cling to Jesus by faith?

18. What warnings should you take from this passage? What can you learn from Judas and the many disciples who fell away?

PRAYER PROMPT

As you close your study of this passage today, thank God for supernaturally and miraculously opening your eyes and heart to the truth of the gospel and the saving work of his Son (if indeed he has done so!). Praise him for allowing you to spiritually feed on Christ—to trust that his body and blood, which were given sacrificially in your place, are your only path to forgiveness and eternal life. Ask him for the courage to cling to the eternal, life-giving words of Jesus—even when they are foolishness in the eyes of the world.

LESSON 9

NOT YET TIME

John 7:1–36

THE BIG PICTURE

We have been seeing that even as his disciples' belief in him is growing, opposition to Jesus is growing as well. The massive claims Jesus has been making about his identity, and the call he has issued for his hearers to place saving faith in him alone, have ultimately led to division; some follow him, and some reject him with increasing vehemence and hatred. This growing opposition to Jesus characterizes John 7:1–36, even as the theme of God's sovereign timing and control becomes increasingly apparent. The passage makes it clear that Jesus will not be delivered up to death until the appointed time.

This entire passage is set during the "Feast of Booths"—a weeklong celebration during which the Jewish people would gather to feast in Jerusalem. As the passage opens, in 7:1–9, Jesus's brothers, who cynically refuse to believe him, confront him and sarcastically encourage him to go to Jerusalem and "show [himself] to the world" (v. 4). At first, Jesus remains where he is, but he then travels to Jerusalem quietly and privately (7:10). As some of the hostile Jews seek to locate him, he suddenly announces his presence by beginning to teach in the temple in Jerusalem. There he declares his unity with God and his insistence on doing the will of the Father—again to mixed reviews and responses (7:11–24).

John then describes in more detail the varied reactions that people at the feast in Jerusalem have to Jesus: some believe that he could indeed be the "Christ"—the Anointed One of God (7:25–26, 31), while others remain cynical... and some even seek to arrest him (7:27–30). The Pharisees and chief priests then make a more formal attempt to send officers to arrest Jesus—an attempt that fails—and the passage ends as the people react to another of Jesus's references to his coming death and resurrection (7:32–36).

Read John 7:1–36.

GETTING STARTED

1. What hostile (or even violent) reactions to the gospel and biblical Christianity have you witnessed from the world today? What seems to motivate such reactions—and what can we learn from them?

2. At what times in your life have you questioned—or been frustrated by—God's timing, providence, or sovereign control? As you look back on those periods, has your opinion of God's timing changed—and, if so, how?

OBSERVING THE TEXT

3. Most scholars believe that about six months pass between the end of John 6 and the beginning of John 7. How could this time gap help to explain people's increasingly hostile reactions to Jesus in this passage?

4. What starkly different reactions to Jesus do we continue to see within this passage? What signs of belief and saving faith do you observe from Jesus's hearers? How do some other people respond to him?

5. What does Jesus continue to reveal in this passage about his identity, his purpose, and the ultimate path his ministry will take? What reference does he make to his death and resurrection?

UNDERSTANDING THE TEXT

6. John 7:1 summarizes the growing (and increasingly violent) hostility that the Jewish leaders show to Jesus. In what way has this hostility escalated? What do you think is motivating their hatred and opposition, based on what you have studied thus far in the gospel of John?

> **Two Kinds of People, pg. 463**
> According to Jesus, the key to recognizing God's truth is not found in a book or taught in a seminary. It is found in our hearts. He says that those who seek to do the will of God will know God's truth when the Word is preached. Notice that all through the Gospels there are two kinds of people. There are those who sit quietly at Jesus' feet to learn. Then there are those like the religious leaders who stand before him, arguing.

7. What do you observe about Jesus's brothers—and about what they say and the attitude they demonstrate to him (7:2–9)? How do they demonstrate cynicism and disbelief—and how does Jesus respond to them? What does Jesus say about *why* the world will hate him (v. 7)?

8. What wisdom and care does Jesus demonstrate as he journeys to Jerusalem for the Feast of Booths (7:10)? Describe the debate that the people who are looking for Jesus in Jerusalem have about his identity (7:11–13).

9. What are the main points of the message and testimony Jesus gives when he appears publicly and begins teaching in the temple (7:14–24)? What seems to be the crowd's general response to Jesus and to his teaching?

Open Hostility, pg. 451
The Feast of Booths might have been a lighthearted time for most Jews, but not for Jesus in this last year of his ministry. John tells us, "The Jews were seeking to kill him" (John 7:1). By "the Jews," John means the religious leaders. Their long, simmering opposition to Jesus had come to a boil, and they now openly sought to take his life.

10. John goes on, in 7:25–31, to describe the people's *divergent* responses to Jesus's teaching. What are they?

11. What seems to motivate the Pharisees' and chief priests' second attempt to arrest Jesus (7:32)? What are the crowds' various mistaken interpretations of Jesus's veiled reference to his death, resurrection, and ascension (7:33–36)?

BIBLE CONNECTIONS

12. Go back to the beginning of the gospel of John and read 1:11–12. How does this lesson's passage illustrate the overview John gives, in his opening chapter, of the way Jesus is received on earth?

13. Read Jesus's lament over Jerusalem in Matthew 23:37–39. What insight does Matthew give us into the emotions Jesus feels regarding the Jewish leaders' angry and cynical response to his ministry?

THEOLOGY CONNECTIONS

14. John explains that the reason Jesus has not yet been arrested and killed (despite the best attempts of the Jewish leaders) is that his "time has not yet come" (7:6; see also v. 30). What does this teach us about the sovereignty, providence, and perfect timing of God? What does Jesus's knowledge of God's timing tell us about his participation in God's sovereign plan—and why is it so important for us to remember this?

15. At least part of the reason for certain people's violent opposition to Jesus in this passage is that he identifies their sin—and their need for repentance (7:7). Answer 17 of the Westminster Shorter Catechism, while speaking about the fall of mankind, explains that "the fall brought mankind into an estate of sin and misery." Why do you think it offends many people in our world today to be told that their natural estate is "sin and misery"—especially if they don't feel that way?

> **A Reason for Hate, pg. 457**
> Above all else, the world hates the cross of Christ. The cross condemns all worldly religion. A Messiah who came to die offends our pride by proclaiming the horror of our sin before God. This is why the Jewish leaders, like many people today, so hated Jesus: "because I testify about it that its works are evil" (John 7:7). Christians will have the same experience that Jesus did. People have varied opinions of Christians, but in general there is rejection and opposition.

APPLYING THE TEXT

16. What do you learn about God's sovereignty and providence in this passage? What encouragement do these lessons offer you to trust in your sovereign God?

17. What can we learn from the boldness and courage Jesus displays by both appearing at the Feast of Booths and speaking words that endanger his life? How could you take steps to follow his example?

18. What lesson should Christians take from this passage about how the world will receive them? Why should we shape our expectations about our own experience around the reception that Jesus receives from the Jewish leaders?

PRAYER PROMPT

As you close your study of this passage from the gospel of John, ask God to continue to soften your heart to be able to put loving, faith-filled belief in Jesus the Messiah—the Anointed One of God. If you believe in him, you should take great joy in the fact that God has opened your heart to faith in his Son—to your everlasting joy and eternal comfort. Pray, further, that God would prepare you to meet hatred and opposition—Jesus was violently opposed, and his people should expect opposition from a sinful world, as well.

LESSON 10

THE LIGHT OF THE WORLD
John 7:37–8:20

THE BIG PICTURE

As the Feast of Booths enters its final day, Jesus stands up during this passage and makes a striking invitation. He urges his hearers to "come to [him] and drink" and declares that "rivers of living water" will flow from the hearts of those who believe in him (7:37–38). While it is not clear precisely which Old Testament Scripture Jesus is referencing here, John explains that he is alluding to the future outpouring of the Holy Spirit on all those who place their faith in him (7:39).

Jesus's bold invitation leads to even more division among the people in Jerusalem: some insist that he is the "Christ," and others question him on the basis of his origin and birthplace—evidently not realizing that he was born in Bethlehem and thus fulfilled the Old Testament's prophecy regarding the Messiah (7:40–44). The chief priests and Pharisees then continue their ferocious opposition to Jesus, despite the reluctance of their officers and a question from one of their own: Nicodemus (7:45–52).

The following confrontation, from 7:53 to 8:11, does not appear in some of the earliest manuscripts of the gospel of John[1]: When the scribes and Pharisees drag before Jesus a woman who has been caught in adultery, he challenges them to affirm their own sinlessness before they put her to

---

1. Although some scholars debate whether this passage should be included in our Bibles, it is likely that John did indeed record this incident.

death. Thwarted, the woman's accusers leave the scene, and Jesus dismisses the woman after calling her to leave her sin behind.

Finally, in 8:12–20, we come to Jesus's next bold "I am" statement, in which he describes himself as the "light of the world" (v. 12). After the Pharisees accuse him of being the only witness regarding his identity, Jesus again affirms that he has the authority to do so and invokes the witness of the Father who sent him. The passage concludes with yet another reminder that Jesus's life and work are under the control of God's sovereign plan and timing (v. 20).

Read John 7:37–8:20.

GETTING STARTED

1. What do you think the Bible means when it says that people who do not know Jesus, and do not believe God's Word, are living in "darkness" (John 8:12)? What behaviors mark the lives of those who live in darkness?

2. Why is it so difficult to move from having a "head" understanding of Jesus to embracing him in our *hearts* as our Savior, our Lord, and our greatest good? Why do we need the Holy Spirit to empower us to do this?

> **The Light of the World, pg. 517**
> Jesus proclaimed, "I am the light of the world." He calls us to believe in him, receiving the light of his free gift of salvation. And then, starting wherever we are right now, we simply begin to follow him as he reveals himself through his Word. And as he leads us out of darkness into light, we will hear him say to us, "You are the light of the world" (Matt. 5:14).

OBSERVING THE TEXT

3. What new statements and claims does Jesus make in this passage about his identity and purpose? What do you think makes these claims so offensive—and frightening—to his Jewish opponents?

4. In this passage, John continues to describe the division among the different responses people have to Jesus. Who in the passage seems to be drawn to Jesus? What evidence do we continue to see that some people have been angrily hardened against him?

5. What do we learn from 7:53–8:11 about Jesus's attitude regarding sinners? Describe the way he reconciles mercy and grace with a refusal to excuse or allow sin.

> **Thirst, pg. 487**
> What a blessing it is to have a thirst for heavenly life, a thirst that will draw you to Jesus and his living water. Jesus stands pleading still, through the preaching of his Word today. How astonishing that he should be the One pleading, when we ought to be on our knees before him. Yet the masses ignore his call, satiated by the polluted waters of earthly pleasure, and feeling no thirst for an entrance into heaven, even as eternity races near.

UNDERSTANDING THE TEXT

6. What need does Jesus identify within human beings (7:37)? What promise does he attach to the invitation he issues in that verse—and how does John say that this promise will ultimately be fulfilled?

7. What confusion grips some of the people as they debate whether Jesus could be the Christ (7:40–44)? What fact do we know, from studying the other gospel accounts, that these people evidently do not?

8. What frustrates the Pharisees about what the officers whom they have sent to arrest Jesus say and do (7:45–49)? Based on what we learned in John 3, why do you think Nicodemus speaks up—and how do the other Pharisees respond to him (7:50–52)?

9. What does John say is the Pharisees' and scribes' intention behind bringing the woman who has been caught in adultery into their midst (7:53–8:6)? What does this reveal about their hearts and about their attitudes and intentions concerning Jesus?

10. How does Jesus respond to the challenge that the scribes and Pharisees issue to him in 8:6–11? What does his simple question to them reveal?

11. What claim does Jesus make about himself with his next "I am" statement, in 8:12? What accusation do the Pharisees bring against him—and what do they base it on (8:13)? What misunderstanding of Jesus's claims about himself and about his relationship with God the Father do they demonstrate next (8:14–20)?

BIBLE CONNECTIONS

12. Go back to John 1, and reread its first five verses. What makes John's imagery regarding light and darkness so powerful and poignant? What spiritual realities are explained and represented to us through this language of light and darkness that both Jesus and John use?

> **Heaven or Hell? pg. 498**
> Like the Continental Divide, which immovably separates the waters of the Pacific from the Atlantic Ocean, Jesus stands eternally as the Divider between the crystal sea of heaven and the sulfurous, flaming lake that is hell. On which side are you? The truth is that every life is flowing to one of these two eternal destinies, depending on faith in Christ or unbelief.

13. Read Isaiah 9:1–4—a passage that Jesus's Jewish listeners would have known. What depth and detail do these verses bring to the claim Jesus makes of being the "light of the world"?

THEOLOGY CONNECTIONS

14. John Calvin explains Jesus's declaration that he is the "light of the world" this way: "By this universal statement he intended to remove the distinction, not only between Jews and Gentiles, but between the learned and ignorant, between persons of distinction and the common people."[2] What is encouraging about who Calvin says can receive Jesus's light?

15. Pascal famously wrote that all human beings have an emptiness, or vacuum, inside them that only God can fill. How does Jesus address this vacuum in the passage for this lesson? What does he say to indicate that he is the answer to human longing and desires?

---

2. John Calvin, *Commentary on the Gospel According to John*, trans. William Pringle (Edinburgh, 1847), 1:324.

APPLYING THE TEXT

16. What tempts you to "thirst" for the things of this world rather than for the eternal blessing and joy that Jesus Christ brings? How can you increase your spiritual thirst for Christ and the things of God?

17. The Pharisees display dramatic hypocrisy as they drag a woman who has been caught in adultery out to be stoned. But lest we are tempted to cast the first stone at them, in turn, what hypocrisies are you guilty of yourself? Why is it important for us to be humble and to repent of our own sins, even as we rightly call out the sinful attitudes and actions of others?

18. How could you more boldly and courageously shine the "light" of Jesus and his gospel into the "darkness" of the world around you? What hope and excitement should we derive from this passage's imagery of light and darkness as we seek to share the good news of Jesus?

PRAYER PROMPT

As you close your study of this passage from the gospel of John, spend some time praising God for the gift of his Son—the "light" of the world, who through the gift of the Holy Spirit provides springs of "living water" to all who believe. Thank God that he has fulfilled all the promises he made to people in a broken and sinful world by sending his Son forth into the darkness of sin, rebellion, and unbelief. Pray for boldness and courage so that you can shine in the world as a "light" for the gospel of Jesus!

LESSON 11

GREATER THAN ABRAHAM

John 8:21–59

THE BIG PICTURE

In this next section of John's gospel, Jesus interacts at length with a group of Jewish leaders—some of whom are evidently starting to believe that he is the Son of God, and others of whom are growing more and more hostile toward him as they reject his claims. As we read, we will see the beauty of Jesus's witness about himself and about his saving purposes for all who believe in him. But we also continue to see the hostility and murderous hatred that rises in the hearts of those who oppose him and who cling instead to their pride, self-righteousness, and human traditions.

Jesus begins by speaking again about his "going away," which refers to his eventual resurrection and return to the Father, only for many of the Jews to again misunderstand him (8:21–23). When they ask him point-blank who he is, Jesus responds with a speech about his relationship with the Father, his role of speaking the word of God, and his purpose of eventually being lifted high in order to secure his people's salvation (8:24–29). We are told that many people believe in Jesus as he bears witness about himself (8:30).

Jesus then begins to speak of the freedom that true disciples enjoy when they believe in him—a statement that offends many of the Jewish listeners who view themselves as already being "free" through their ethnic heritage (8:31–38). The confrontation ramps up in intensity as Jesus responds to the Jews' claim that Abraham is their father by asserting that, actually, the "devil" is their father—if they refuse to listen to and believe in Jesus (8:39–47).

As his Jewish opponents continue to challenge his claims (and his implication that he is greater than Abraham), their confrontation culminates in one final, grand claim from Jesus: he makes yet another "I am" statement by affirming that, even before Abraham was, "I am" (8:48–58). The Jews have heard enough—they pick up stones to kill Jesus, but he hides himself and leaves the temple (8:59).

Read John 8:21–59.

GETTING STARTED

1. In what ways do people deceive themselves into thinking they are "okay" with God, instead of recognizing that they need to repent and experience a massive change of mind and heart?

2. What are some potential ways you could tell whether someone is a true *disciple* of Jesus or is merely *interested* in some aspects of Christianity? Which of Jesus's claims might make the second type of person uncomfortable?

A Dreadful Sermon, pg. 536
Luther described this passage as "a dreadful sermon," and it was. Jesus spoke of his opponents' seeking but not finding and dying in their sins. But the sermon's result was glorious, just as the preaching of Jesus is mighty and glorious today. John tells us how: "As he was saying these things, many believed in him" (John 8:30).

OBSERVING THE TEXT

3. What claims does Jesus make about his identity and purpose throughout this passage? What connections does he draw between himself and God the Father? Which of his claims are most offensive to his Jewish opponents?

4. John makes it clear in this passage that some of Jesus's hearers truly believe in him, through his preaching and teaching, even as others oppose him more and more violently. What makes this encouraging—and what other encouraging details do you see in this passage?

5. What elements of Jesus's sermon seem harsh? What can we learn about Jesus from them?

> **A Warning to the Pharisees, pg. 551**
> This was meant as a warning to the Pharisees. Before them stood the true and eternal Son of God. If they continued to oppose him, they would be cast out with no hope of salvation, regardless of their human lineage. Only by receiving their freedom through faith in Jesus, as Abraham and Isaac had done by trusting God's promises, would they gain the rights of true sons.

UNDERSTANDING THE TEXT

6. What hints does Jesus leave in John 8:21–29 about his death, resurrection, and ascension? What do his listeners say to demonstrate that not all of them understand his meaning—and why do you think this is the case?

7. What happens in the hearts of some of Jesus's listeners, while many are rejecting his message (8:30)? What does Jesus say to these people (8:31–32)?

8. What does John 8:33 show that Jesus's Jewish opponents are basing their hope on? How does Jesus respond to their hope (8:34–38)?

9. What two claims do the Jews make in 8:39–41 about who their "father" is—and what do these claims reveal about their self-perception? Who does Jesus identify to be their true "father" in 8:42–47? What devastating conclusions does he draw about their spiritual condition?

10. As Jesus makes further claims regarding Abraham, what are the Jews next offended about (8:48–56)? What makes it obvious to them that Jesus is placing himself *above* Abraham in terms of his significance and authority (v. 56)?

11. What claim does Jesus make in 8:58—and what does this statement imply? What is the Jews' response to it, and why do you think this would have finally driven them to this point? How does 8:59 reveal that God's sovereign and perfect timing regarding Jesus's crucifixion remains in control?

BIBLE CONNECTIONS

12. The same Jesus who is "gentle and lowly" is also the one who tells unbelieving religious leaders that their father is the devil! Read Matthew 11:28–30. What beautiful invitation does Jesus issue in those verses? What makes the harsh words of rebuke that he delivers to his Jewish opponents, in this lesson's passage, consistent with the gracious character he reveals through his invitation from Matthew 11?

13. Read Galatians 3:6–9. What does Paul say it means to be a true child of Abraham? What agreement do you see between what Paul says here and what Jesus teaches about Abraham in our passage for this lesson? How does Paul apply that teaching?

THEOLOGY CONNECTIONS

14. Jesus's Jewish opponents were trusting, as descendants of Abraham, that their ethnic lineage would bring them favor with God—not realizing that they were sinners in need of repentance and spiritual rebirth. How can this passage serve as a warning to those who have grown up in the church and under Christian families, traditions, and teaching?

15. Answer 18 of the Westminster Shorter Catechism explains that the doctrine of total depravity leads to "the corruption of [man's] whole nature, which is commonly called Original Sin, together with all actual transgressions which proceed from it." How does Jesus confirm the truth of this doctrine in our passage for this lesson?

APPLYING THE TEXT

16. What can you learn from this passage about the character of Jesus—and specifically about the things he is concerned about? Why do you think he confronts certain attitudes with the vehemence and frankness that we see here?

17. Based on what you see in this passage, do you think Jesus would confront you about any attitudes you hold regarding your salvation? Why or why not? What attitudes does this passage remind you that you should have instead?

18. What different responses does this passage remind you that you should anticipate when you share the gospel? What makes doctrines such as the exclusivity of Christ, or total depravity, so offensive to many people today?

Tested, Experienced, and Blessed, pg. 544
True discipleship is tested and proved by abiding in the Word of Christ. True discipleship is experienced as our lives are increasingly enlightened in the truth of Christ's Word. This true discipleship is then blessed through this same truth. Jesus concluded, "If you abide in my word, you are truly my disciples, and you will know the truth, and the truth will set you free" (John 8:31–32).

PRAYER PROMPT

Jesus's words to his Jewish opponents in this passage are piercing, powerful, and harsh—he does not allow them to remain in their dangerous self-righteous and self-deceived spiritual state! As you close your study of this passage, ask God to help you to allow his Word to shape your understanding of Jesus, his Son—and of what it means to be his disciple. Pray for the humility to be able to receive the gospel with repentance and faith as you trust in the Son alone to be your righteousness and goodness.

LESSON 12

BLINDNESS TO SIGHT

John 9:1–41

THE BIG PICTURE

As Richard Phillips points out in his commentary, John 9 begins a distinctly new section of the book.[1] Over the next three chapters of this gospel, we will see how Jesus specifically encourages and ministers personally to those who believe in him—even as he continues to march toward his sacrificial death on the cross and resurrection from the dead. In the passage for this lesson, John hones in on Jesus's encounters with a man who has been born blind—and the continuing vehement opposition from some Jewish leaders in the wake of this man's physical healing and spiritual rebirth.

The narrative begins as Jesus's disciples ask him about the sin that they assume caused a man, whom they are passing by, to be blind from birth—was it, they ask, committed by the man or his parents (9:1–2)? Jesus tells them that this man's blindness is instead an opportunity for God to show his great works through Jesus, and he then miraculously heals him (9:3–7). Scarcely able to believe that he is the same man who was formerly blind, the bystanders question him repeatedly (9:8–12).

As the Pharisees pick up the investigation, John adds an important detail: that Jesus has performed this healing on the Sabbath day (9:13–14). Some of the Pharisees interpret this as a violation of the Sabbath law—even as

---

1. See Richard D. Phillips, *John*, vol. 1, *Chapters 1–10* (Phillipsburg, NJ: P&R Publishing, 2014), 576.

some question how such a wonderful healing could be sinful (9:15–17). The Pharisees then summon the blind man's parents, who cautiously and fearfully urge the Jewish leaders to allow their son to speak for himself (9:18–23). When the Pharisees question the man again, an intense interaction follows (9:24–34). The formerly blind man pushes back against the Jewish leaders as he bears witness to the healing that has taken place and implies that Jesus has truly been sent from God (v. 33). The Jewish leaders then angrily cast the man out (v. 34).

The passage concludes as Jesus returns to the man he has healed and identifies himself as the Son of Man; he then encourages the man and receives his belief and worship . . . even as the Pharisees continue to display *their* spiritual blindness through their disbelief and their disdain for Jesus (9:35–41).

Read John 9:1–41.

GETTING STARTED

1. Give an example of a single action you have taken that has produced at least two very different responses from different kinds of people. Why did the people who were involved respond to your action in those ways?

2. Have you ever seen someone's attention to detail cause him or her to miss a larger and more important perspective? What leads people to get so caught up with trivial rules that they miss a task or mission's big-picture context—or even its purpose?

OBSERVING THE TEXT

3. At what points in this passage do you see Jesus demonstrating tenderness? At what points does he show toughness? What is he continuing to teach us about his character—and about the kind of person whom he welcomes with open arms?

4. Why do many of the Pharisees continue to oppose Jesus? What aspects of his ministry and teaching make them the most angry and defensive?

5. What signs do you see in this passage that some people are beginning to believe in Jesus? What obstacles do they face?

> **Leading Many to the Light, pg. 584**
> "As long as I am in the world," Jesus said, "I am the light of the world" (John 9:5). He illustrated this by opening the eyes of the man who had been born blind. It was a picture of his whole ministry. During his three years of ministering on earth, Jesus displayed the light of God to the world, and through his saving work he led many to his light.

UNDERSTANDING THE TEXT

6. What assumptions do the disciples make about what causes disability or suffering—and what differing perspective does Jesus introduce to them (9:1–4)? How does the miraculous healing that he performs in 9:6–7 help to illustrate the claim he makes about himself in 9:5?

7. What attitude seems to characterize those who question the formerly blind man in 9:8–12? What makes it obvious that the Pharisees who question the man in 9:13–17 are doing so with a more cynical and bitter attitude? While many of the Pharisees still angrily oppose Jesus, what do some of them begin to wonder about him?

8. What does the fact that the Pharisees see this healing Jesus has performed as being a violation of Sabbath law (9:14–16) reveal about their hearts (and about the way they have misunderstood God's heart)?

9. What is the Pharisees' purpose behind calling the blind man's parents (9:18–19)? What risk do the parents face if they confess Jesus to be the Christ, and how do they feel about this risk (9:20–23)?

10. The Pharisees then confront and question the formerl[y blind man] again—and what do they seem to try to convince him, wh[at do they say] (9:24–29)? What do we learn about the man's personali[ty and faith] from his response to them (9:30–33)? How do the Pharisees react to what he says—and why (9:34)?

11. What does Jesus do to encourage and strengthen the genuine faith of the man he has healed (9:35–38)? What spiritual condition does Jesus again identify that the Pharisees have, and what are its implications (9:39–41)?

BIBLE CONNECTIONS

12. Read Isaiah 35:4–6. How does the passage that we are studying show this prophecy being beautifully fulfilled? What does this prophecy tell us that its fulfillment signifies?

Work Redefined, pg. 596

Jesus did not violate God's law, but only that of the Pharisees. God's law taught that on the seventh day, "You shall not do any work" (Ex. 20:10). But the Pharisees took it upon themselves to define in minute detail what was and was not "work," spelling out thirty-nine categories of activities that they said violated the Sabbath.

13. Read Luke 13:1–5. What more does Jesus teach us about the deeper purposes God has for suffering and tragedy? What response does Jesus tell his disciples that people should have to seeing disaster or suffering?

THEOLOGY CONNECTIONS

14. The doctrine of *total depravity*, which our last lesson discussed, leads naturally to the doctrine of *regeneration*, which describes how a sinful heart is miraculously awakened so that it can believe and have saving faith. How is the need for regeneration illustrated by this passage, on both a physical and a spiritual level?

15. The Westminster Confession of Faith explains the Sabbath day by saying that God, "in his Word, by a positive, moral, and perpetual commandment, binding all men in all ages . . . hath particularly appointed one day in seven for a Sabbath, to be kept holy unto him" (21.7). In what way were Jesus's actions in our passage for this lesson keeping the Sabbath day holy, despite the Pharisees' objections? What lessons could we learn from this passage about how we ought to treat the Sabbath?

APPLYING THE TEXT

16. Since John chooses only seven of Jesus's many miracles to record in his gospel, what specific reason do you think he had for recording and describing *this* one in particular? In what way does this healing serve as a picture of Jesus's entire ministry—and of his purpose for coming into the world?

17. How do the Pharisees' human traditions clash with the healing and saving work God is performing through Jesus? Have you seen human traditions—perhaps even those of the church—threaten to do the same today? If so, how did this play out?

18. What can we learn from the healed man about how to walk in faith? Do you respond to Jesus the same way he did? What is this passage showing you that you might need to change in your behavior or attitude?

> **Seven Miracles, pg. 585**
> There are only seven [miracles recorded by John]. . . . These were not the only miracles witnessed by John, but they were selected to teach us about the nature of the salvation that Jesus came to give.

PRAYER PROMPT

This passage should prompt us to see ourselves, by God's grace, as formerly blind sinners who have been given spiritual sight and life through Jesus—the "light" of the world. If God has done this work in you, by the power of the Holy Spirit, then praise him! Ask him for grace and strength so that you can point others who are walking in blindness to the light of the gospel of Jesus Christ and to saving belief in the Son.

LESSON 13

THE GOOD SHEPHERD

John 10:1–42

THE BIG PICTURE

In John 10, we come to teaching from Jesus that is structured around two new "I am" statements; he presents himself as both the "good shepherd" and the "door" for his sheep. The "good shepherd" was highly anticipated in the Old Testament—particularly in Ezekiel 34, in which God condemns the abusive shepherds of his people and promises to be, himself, his people's eternal good and their kind shepherd.

Jesus begins by alluding to the shepherd metaphor, but he is met with confusion from his listeners (10:1–6). He then becomes more explicit, identifying himself as the "door" and then as the "good shepherd" (10:7–11). He goes on to explain that these roles have been given to him by the Father—and that they will require his sacrificial death on behalf of the sheep (10:12–18). His teaching causes further confusion and division among the Jewish leaders and other listeners (10:19–21).

The next verse places the scene during the Feast of Dedication in Jerusalem (10:22), where Jesus continues to describe himself as the saving shepherd who will offer eternal life to his sheep (10:23–28). And not only is this true, but he further states that he is "one" with the Father (10:29–30). This causes the Jews to pick up stones in yet another failed attempt to kill him (10:31).

The passage ends with Jesus demanding to know which of his good works have led the Jews to intend to murder him; they explain that they want to stone him because he has claimed to be equal with the Father (10:32–33). Jesus again insists that he is acting and speaking on God's behalf, and he invites the Jews to believe in him (10:34–39). John concludes this passage by showing us that "many" do indeed believe in Jesus (10:40–42).

Read John 10:1–42.

GETTING STARTED

1. What behaviors and attitudes mark Christian leaders or pastors as being abusive? What are the devastating consequences of their abuse—both for Christians and for unbelieving observers?

2. We are often tempted to soften our insistence that Jesus is the only way to salvation—what are some forms that this can take, and why do we feel the temptation to do it?

OBSERVING THE TEXT

3. What attitudes does this passage demonstrate that Jesus feels toward his "sheep"? How do these attitudes contrast with his stance toward the Pharisees and Jewish leaders who reject him?

4. What differing reactions to Jesus do we see in this passage? How does John describe the rejection, the belief, and the ongoing confusion that different people experience after interacting with Jesus?

5. In this passage, Jesus becomes even more explicit about his identity and the salvation he will accomplish through his sacrificial death. What words and phrases does he use to express these things?

UNDERSTANDING THE TEXT

6. In the opening verses of this passage, what figure of speech does Jesus introduce to describe his coming and purpose—and how do his listeners respond to it (10:1–6)? Why do you think he introduces this metaphor more vaguely, at the outset, like this?

God's Plan, pg. 647
Not only did God know that Jesus was going to die, but he permitted it to happen. And not only did he permit it to happen, but he planned it. . . . And according to that same plan, Jesus rose from the dead to give eternal life to his sheep. So not only did Jesus die for us, but it was also for us that God gave his divine Son.

7. What two "I am" statements does Jesus make in 10:7–13—and what does he say is significant about them? What does it mean for Jesus to be the "good shepherd"? What does it mean for him to say he is the "door"?

8. Read 10:19–21, and then look ahead to 10:40–42. What questions do many people have about Jesus—and what do these questions reveal about their thinking?

9. What does Jesus say that he will do for his "sheep" (10:14–18)? What does he say to indicate that his people will be made up of believers who are outside the community of Israel (see v. 16)? What does he say to indicate that he is not a helpless victim of the events that will take place (vv. 17–18)?

> **One Road to God's Grace, pg. 627**
> [Some people] demand another way—any other way—that grants a salvation that is to their own glory instead of to God's. Such people delight to insist that many roads lead to God, which is true. But only one of those roads leads to his forgiving grace instead of his judgment. When it comes to salvation, Jesus insists, "I am the door."

10. During the Feast of Dedication in Jerusalem, what claims does Jesus again make to the Jews as they surround him and question him about his identity (10:22–30)? What does he insist about the relationship between himself and God the Father? What does he explain about the authority he holds and the role he plays in the salvation of men and women?

11. As the Jews pick up stones to kill him (10:31), how does Jesus expose the true source of their murderous hatred toward him (10:32–33)? Why is it important for us to understand that the Jews are offended because of Jesus's *claims* rather than because of the *works* he performs? On what basis does Jesus call them to accept his claims—and his connection to the Father—and come to him in belief (10:34–39)?

BIBLE CONNECTIONS

12. Jesus's declaration that he is the "good shepherd" is rich with Old Testament connotations. Skim through Ezekiel 34:1–16. What is God's response to the "shepherds" of his people who have been abusive and selfish to Israel throughout its history? What great promise does he make—and how will Jesus ultimately fulfill this promise?

13. Read Psalm 23, to which Ezekiel 34 seems to allude. How do Jesus's death, resurrection, and eternal reign beautifully fulfill the promises of this psalm? What hope can you take from this picture of God—even when following Jesus leads you through hardship and suffering?

THEOLOGY CONNECTIONS

14. Jesus's presentation of himself as the "door" invokes the doctrine of the *exclusivity of Christ*. This doctrine affirms that Jesus *alone* is the way to salvation—that sinners receive eternal life only by repenting and putting their faith in him as their Savior and Lord. Why is it so important for God's people to cling to this doctrine? What often makes it an offensive and unpopular doctrine in our world today?

> **Building Power or Teaching the Ways of God? pg. 618**
> In Jesus' day, the Pharisees misused the law to build their own power on the foundation of works-righteousness. In our day, false shepherds employ the tactics of Hollywood, with its glittering entertainment, and Madison Avenue, employing the subtle manipulations of the advertising firms, to win large followings. But a true shepherd will stick to the ways of God as taught in the Bible.

15. This passage shows us again that Jesus's death was part of God's sovereign plan (see 10:18). As the Westminster Confession of Faith explains, "God, the great Creator of all things, upholds, directs, disposes, and governs all creatures, actions, and things, from the greatest even to the least, by his most wise and holy providence" (5.1). What evidence can you offer that even the death of Jesus is included within God's providential plan?

APPLYING THE TEXT

16. Why should it bring great comfort to Christians that Jesus identifies himself as the "good shepherd"? How have you seen him demonstrate his shepherding love and care for you—in both eternal and temporal ways?

17. What strength does this passage have to offer for our resolve and for our insistence on lovingly and humbly presenting Jesus as the only way for every man, woman, and child to find salvation?

18. Although the phrase "the good shepherd" applies primarily to Jesus, the passage we studied in this lesson has strong implications for the way his under-shepherds (pastors, Christian leaders, and so on) should care for God's people. What are some of these? What can pastors learn from the "good shepherd" concerning their teaching and preaching, attitude toward God's people, and general demeanor?

PRAYER PROMPT

This passage ought to fill our hearts with joy and cause them to trust and feel secure in Jesus—if we have indeed hidden ourselves in him by faith. He is our Great Shepherd who has laid down his life in order to save us and to bring us into the eternal care of the Father's hand! Today, praise Jesus for the sacrificial love and care he has shown you and thank him for being your eternally Good Shepherd who will care for you and complete the good work that he began in you once you put your faith in him.

Jon Nielson is senior pastor of Christ Presbyterian Church in Wheaton, Illinois, and the author of *Bible Study: A Student's Guide*, among other books. He has served in pastoral positions at several churches in Illinois—including Holy Trinity Church in Chicago, College Church in Wheaton, and Spring Valley Presbyterian Church in Roselle—and as director of training for the Charles Simeon Trust.

Richard D. Phillips (MDiv, Westminster Theological Seminary; DD, Greenville Presbyterian Theological Seminary) is the senior minister of Second Presbyterian Church of Greenville, South Carolina. He is a council member of the Alliance of Confessing Evangelicals and of The Gospel Coalition and chairman of the Philadelphia Conference on Reformed Theology.

Did you enjoy this Bible study? Consider writing a review online. The authors appreciate your feedback!

Or write to P&R at editorial@prpbooks.com with your comments. We'd love to hear from you.

P&R PUBLISHING'S COMPANION COMMENTARY

Richard Phillips's two-volume commentary on John reflects the Reformed Expository Commentary series's commitment to thorough, Calvinistic, redemptive-historical, and expositional teaching of the biblical text. Discover the apostle John's chief focus on the deity of Christ, the gospel witness of the church, and salvation through faith in Jesus. Although scholarly, it explains doctrines lucidly, communicates in nontechnical language, and applies each passage to the reader's life.

The Reformed Expository Commentary (REC) series is accessible to both pastors and lay readers. Each volume in the series provides exposition that gives careful attention to the biblical text, is doctrinally Reformed, focuses on Christ through the lens of redemptive history, and applies the Bible to our contemporary setting.

Praise for the Reformed Expository Commentary Series

"Well-researched and well-reasoned, practical and pastoral, shrewd, solid, and searching." —**J. I. Packer**

"A rare combination of biblical insight, theological substance, and pastoral application." —**Al Mohler**

"Here, rigorous expository methodology, nuanced biblical theology, and pastoral passion combine." —**R. Kent Hughes**